PREFACE

How could a healthy, young American woman, who sailed to China on a comfortable ocean liner, be returned in a prisoner exchange seven years later as a Japanese prisoner of war, one of a company described by the American Medical Authorities as, "the largest group of the most emaciated Americans they had ever seen?"

MARTHA PHILIPS — Missionary to China.

BEHIND STONE WALLS and BARBED WIRE

by
Martha Philips
and
Mary Hadden

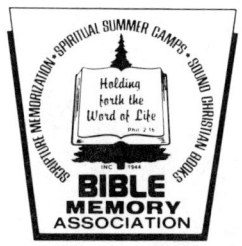

Bible Memory Association

P. O. Box 12,000 • Ringgold, LA 71068-2000
(318) 894-9154

Copyright © 1991 by Bible Memory Association.
All rights reserved.
No portion of this book may be reproduced without permission.
ISBN 0-89323-057-X

INTRODUCTION

I first met Martha Philips at Bible Memory Association camp at Ringgold, Louisiana. That summer, 1981, she was teaching Bible lessons with a missionary emphasis to teens.

It was exciting to hear her accounts of events that happened on the mission field.

"Have you ever written any of this in a book for others to read?" I asked.

"No," she answered. "When I was young, I did not have time; I was on a heavy schedule. Now I have time but I cannot see." (Martha is now legally blind and has only peripheral vision.)

I heard a still small voice say, "You do it." For several days I argued: "I can't." "I am not a writer." "I can't even type decently." But when I gave in to the Spirit's leading, I felt great peace and joy.

This little book is the result of that leading. It is compiled from Martha's diaries, which the Lord preserved for her when she was repatriated from China, from her letters to her parents and from her memories.

Even in her mid-eighties, Martha still traveled, telling of God's faithfulness. People sat enthralled, on the edges of their seats, as she told the story of how God led her to the mission field in China and of His care for His children in trying times. It seemed that everyone wanted to hear her "Concentration Camp Story."

She and I have not chosen to dwell on the difficulties and sufferings. They were there, but many others have told of the experiences they suffered while interned in concentration camps showing "man's inhumanity to man." We have chosen to tell of the loving Father who is always there, always faithful and ready to deliver His children when the going is rough.

We want Christians to remember that God has not promised an easy life. Our Lord Himself says that in this life we shall have tribulation; but He has promised that He will never leave us nor forsake us. He is always there. He will not allow the testing to be greater than we can bear. The hard things He allows to come upon us are designed to help us to grow spiritually – to shape the Christian into His image.

Therefore, yield yourself to the Lord; be obedient to His leading. Learn to say with Paul – "I can do all things through Christ who strengthens me."

Mary Hadden

CONTENTS

PART ONE - A DREAM FULFILLED

1. Across the Pacific 9
2. China at Last 22
3. Yangchow 29
4. The School at Chefoo 41

PART TWO - IN THE WAR BUT NOT OF IT

5. Fall of Peking 52
6. Fall of Chefoo 57
7. The Russian Work 67
8. Peace in the Face of War 74

PART THREE - UNDER HOUSE ARREST

9. Under House Arrest 79
10. Financial Problems 87
11. What is God Doing? 96

PART FOUR - INTERNED!

12. Temple Hill 101
13. Adjusting 111
14. More Glimpses of Camp Life 121
15. A Consecration Camp 126
16. God Sends Us to Weihsien 130

PART FIVE - GOING HOME

17. Our Trip to Shanghai 139
18. The Teia Maru 145
19. On the Luxurious Gripsholm 153

PART SIX - OUR FAITHFUL GOD

20. Back to the States 161
21. A New Commission 168

A DREAM FULFILLED

C·H·A·P·T·E·R

1

ACROSS THE PACIFIC DESTINATION – CHINA
September – October, 1936

Details of my voyage across the Pacific are indelibly etched upon my memory. My heart was filled with joy as I boarded the Japanese ship in Victoria, British Columbia, Canada, on September 12, 1936, bound for Shanghai. I was on the way to China after years of preparation for the mission field, the fulfillment of the call of God.

The ship carried a cargo of flour and railroad iron destined for Yokohama, but more important, on this trip, she was a **missionary ship**.

Among the hundreds of passengers were three groups of missionaries bound for China – workers for **The South China Boat Mission, The Door of Hope Mission,** and about twenty new missionaries for **China Inland Mission.** Other missionaries were going to Japan, India and Africa. We enjoyed rich fellowship with one another for we were all setting forth to carry out God's Great Commission – **"Go ye into all the world and**

N. Y. K. Line — M. S. Heian Maru 11,600 tons bound for China.

Here we are, clad in our "life belts," aboard ship.

preach the gospel to every creature." (Mark 16:15)

We realized we were going into a dangerous situation. In 1934 John and Betty Stam, missionaries with China Inland Mission, had been slain on the mission field by Chinese bandits. The political situation was turbulent. Much violence went on over the countryside; so no one went to the mission field in China in 1935. We, who went in 1936, were the first to go since the deaths of the Stams. We knew the same could happen to us, but if it did we would be with the Lord. We trusted Him for His protection and leading.

The Japanese officers on our ship were courteous and considerate of our welfare and comfort. They did everything they could to make the trip pleasant for us.

I marveled at the beauty of the ocean as we walked about, or sat in chairs on the deck. The sea was constantly changing and restless, but always beautiful, even in the face of a storm. At times, great swells rocked the ship. Sometimes huge waves rolled and crashed onto themselves, leaving behind ever-changing mountains and valleys of water and foam. Spray from the waves often washed over the deck. It all gave a vivid picture of Isaiah 57:20,21 **"...the wicked are like the troubled sea, when it cannot rest, whose waters cast up mire and dirt. There is no peace, saith my God, to the wicked."**

I gained a clearer understanding of the expression "pouring oil on troubled water" on this trip. One day the sea had an oily look on the surface which, the seamen say, always means a typhoon is about to strike – but this time it did not. Though the surface of the water was as smooth as glass, without even a ripple, an occasional upheaval erupted to the surface in the form of a gigantic swell, indicating great pressure and unrest below.

We passed through the edges of two typhoons, but God's hand protected this ship and no harm was done to it. Other ships in the same shipping lane were caught by the fury of the storms and were damaged.

One afternoon as we neared the Japanese port of Yokohama, the captain invited some of us up to the bridge to see the sun set behind the mountains of Japan. We had seen land, the Aleutian Islands, in the distance for half the day. The scene was fascinating. We looked down at the water, then across to the mountains and the sun setting behind them. The rosy glow across the horizon was exquisitely beautiful. How can anyone look at the beauty God has created and deny Him?

The next morning while our ship lay anchored in the harbor before it actually docked, a Japanese fishing fleet sailed out past us. The little oriental sailboats made a lovely picture silhouetted against the rose-gray sky of dawn.

As our ship came near the dock, we saw many people waiting. There were beautiful Japanese girls in lovely kimonos, and modern Japanese men dressed in European clothes. Some children were in Japanese, some in foreign clothes. Coolies were clad in the traditional garb of anything they could find, with a funny kimono-like shirt thrown over all.

When the gangplank was lowered, that crowd swarmed onto the ship. Then the fun began.

Tokyo Memorial Temple — The memorial to the 50,000 who lost their lives in the earthquake of Japan. The spirits of these people are worshipped here.

In a Japanese garden in Tokyo. Miss Lang and I are near the center of the picture.

Each Japanese seemed to try to out-do the one he was greeting in the extremity of bowing. I watched one passenger as he greeted a man from shore. He bowed once; the second bow was deeper. The third time, his head was near his knees. While he was suspended in mid-air in that bent-over position, he sneaked a glance from the corner of his eye. Seeing that his competitor was lower than he, he arose, and with great aplomb, bowed still lower. He was not going to be out-done! (I was glad I had on a suit with full sleeves that hid my grins and giggles until I reached my state-room.)

We went ashore, finally, amid tooting horns, ringing bells and all sorts of bids for our money.

We were scheduled to spend two and one half days in the port city of Yokohama while the cargo of flour and iron was being unloaded. Then this ship was to take us to the other side of the island where we were to board our next ship.

The next day the general passenger agent of the shipping line provided a sightseeing tour in Tokyo for the twenty China Inland Mission people. We rode a quaint little electric train (it reminded me of a cracker box) from Yokohama to Tokyo. It was an express train that passed up all the stops made by the other trains. Once this train got going, it had the rock and sway of a galloping horse. We found it both amusing and pleasant.

The agent met us in Tokyo and loaded us into taxis. We rode through a Japanese market where everything was displayed on the street. We saw the empty beauty of a Buddhist temple. Our taxis carried us through a lovely Japanese garden where we were encouraged to take pictures.

We were often told, "You may take pictures here." We were just as often told suddenly, "Now, put your cameras away." One individual, who was slow to respond, snapped a picture in a forbidden area. The Japanese guide immediately snatched the camera, opened it and removed the film. He held it up to the sunlight and innocently observed, "Hm-m! No picture on this!"

We were properly impressed by that and learned that cameras must be put away when we were told. (We wondered later what secret war preparations were going on in that area in 1936. The war did not begin until December, 1941.) We were faced with such control the whole time we were in Japan.

Our guide took us to see the Buddhist Memorial Temple – a memorial of the fifty thousand people who died in the earthquake of 1923.

We went past the Imperial Palace which was surrounded by a high stone wall and a wide, deep moat. Tourists were not allowed to enter, but what we could see was beautiful.

It was about 12:00 or 12:30 P.M. when we passed by the baseball stadium. A game was to begin at 2:00 P.M. and already hundreds of bicycles were neatly parked – two hours before the game was to begin. More were coming in from every direction. Cars were rushing in, two and three abreast. Anyone going against that traffic, as we were, had to remain in a single lane.

Heavily laden ox-carts moved slowly and deliberately through the streets, utterly oblivious to the fast-moving cars, bicycles, and other traffic. A few thin, sway-backed horses pulled wagons or carts. Each horse had a tub of chopped hay

Buddhist temple in Tokyo.

This drawing is much like the rickshaw I rode in.

hanging from his harness. Whenever the horse was stopped, his tub of hay was placed before him and he had refreshment until time to move on.

There were bicycles with heavily over-loaded trailers, often propelled by a small boy. There were rickshas, coolies with carrying poles, now and then a man, a woman or a child pulling a cart. All were oblivious of anyone else.

They really had a neat way of enforcing traffic laws. Anyone who violated a traffic ordinance was immediately stopped by an officer who simply took away the driver's license. Nothing slow about that!

It was raining very hard before we got back to Yokohama – so hard it had been impossible to unload the large cargo of flour from the ship. It was clear that we would have to go by rail across this largest island of Japan, a full day's journey, to Kobe if we were to make connections with our next ship.

The officials told us that all our baggage must go through Japanese customs. Everything must be unpacked in the presence of Japanese Customs Inspectors, then repacked. At Victoria, British Columbia, everything had been thoroughly inspected by Japanese Customs Officials. Our chaperon tried to persuade them that our baggage need not be inspected again, since we had neither seen nor opened it in Japan. They continued to insist it must be inspected.

There was only one thing to do. We committed it to the Lord. While we were at the dinner table that night, our chaperon received a note from Customs Officials saying they would **bond** our baggage through Japan. Only our hand luggage which we had used in Japan need be inspected.

Those officials told us there would be an excess baggage charge in addition to the express train charge of four yen apiece because the fast train cost more. Then the shipping company surprised us and paid for both. They even gave us our train tickets plus thirty yen each to buy our meals on the train. The Lord certainly took care of every detail.

The next morning, as we were leaving Yokohama for Kobe, we were each given a booklet describing our overland tour and a time table telling what we could expect to see at each moment. For example: – 10:45 – Cormorant Fishing. At that exact time we saw a man in a fishing boat. His cormorant was tied so he could fish but not escape. A band around his neck kept the bird from swallowing the fish he caught. At just the right moment, the bird dived off the boat, caught a fish and returned to his master. The man reached inside the bird's beak, removed the fish and tossed it into his basket. What a demonstration of perfect timing!

"You can set your watch by our electric trains," the Japanese advertised. Their huge railway service was, indeed, well scheduled and efficient – on time to the minute. **The trains left on time whether the passengers were aboard or not.**

When we reached the train station in Kobe, we could see the ships in the harbor. Our ship, the Shanghai Maru, was a coal burner. She was smaller than the oil burning vessel that had carried us across the Pacific.

We couldn't believe our eyes as we watched the refueling of that ship. Scores of tiny Japanese women, each carrying a bag of coal slung over her

The Shanghai Maru near Kobe.

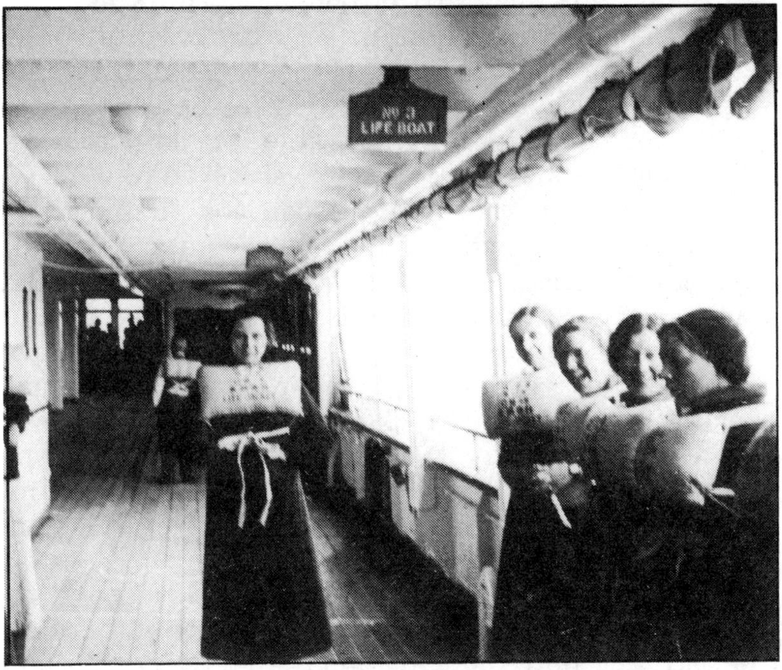

Part of our group in life jackets, for boat drill.

shoulders and hanging down her back, climbed up the side of the ship. Each emptied her bag of coal and returned for another load, over and over, until the coal bins were full. Those women looked like a swarm of ants climbing up and down the hull of the ship. (Women, you see, are the workhorses of Japan.)

That evening we went shopping on the main street of Kobe. The strange little oriental shops opened right onto the street, and the people were determined that we should buy.

It seemed strange to see the crowds walking in the street; but there was no other place to walk. There were no sidewalks. The street was too narrow for cars. There were bicycles and a few rickshas, but most of the people were on foot.

We spent that night in a lovely oriental hotel, courtesy of the shipping line. The Lord had arranged every detail of our trip far better than we could have. He is truly able to do exceeding abundantly above all we can ask or think.

We had another real reason for thanksgiving concerning the change of our route. It was typhoon season and ships were having a rough time in the storms. Our inland trip spared us that danger. If our cargo of flour and iron had been removed as scheduled, a typhoon would have tossed our ship about like a straw.

The Lord knew about all the problems beforehand and planned for us this lovely overland trip that many people travel hundreds of miles and pay large sums of money to see.

The next morning, after a good rest in the hotel, we boarded our ship, the Shanghai Maru, bound for Shanghai. As we crossed Japan's inland sea, the water was so calm there was scarcely a ripple.

We watched the sun, a great ball of fire, go down behind the mountains. It reminded me of Deception Pass in Washington State, only this channel was wider and there were more islands.

The mountains were rugged and unusual. In a quiet cove where we might have built one house, there was often a whole village. Terraced farms on the hillside provided food for the families and their livestock. The whole scene was as beautiful as a picture postcard.

CHAPTER 2

CHINA AT LAST
October, 1936

Our ship the Shanghai Maru carried us from Kobe to Shanghai. **I was in China at last!** I looked about in wonder and took in the strange sights, sounds and smells. When at last, the gangplank was lowered, I joined the excited passengers as they walked off the ship. Representatives from South China Boat Mission, Door of Hope Mission and China Inland Mission were there to meet their new workers and to help them through customs. We collected our baggage and went to our respective headquarters.

We of China Inland Mission were glad to reach the CIM Headquarters which was to be our home for the next few days. We talked far into the night. At last we retired to our own rooms and to bed.

I was too excited to sleep. My mind kept going over the leading of the Lord that had brought me to China.

When, as a child, I read "Go ye into all the world and preach the gospel to every creature," it

Part of the China Inland Mission's Headquarters, located in the international settlement at Shanghai, 1936.

seemed that God was speaking directly to me. I was nine years old at the time, but I knew, even then, that God wanted me to be a missionary. By the time I was ten, I understood that He wanted me to go to China.

I knew that when Jesus said, "If you love me, keep my commandments," He meant that the proof of one's love for Him was obedience. Even as a small child I knew that I loved Jesus and wanted to please Him.

I also learned Colossians 3:20 – "Children obey your parents..." I remember well a lesson Mother taught me. I was always obedient; I always did as I was told – when I got ready. One day when I had done something I wanted to do first, before doing what Mother had told me to do, she sat me down and said, "Martha, delayed obedience is disobedience." She went on to explain that if I did as I wanted first, I was not being obedient at all.

I understood then that delayed obedience really was disobedience. I learned to obey immediately, and to do what I wanted later. This lesson stayed with me and through the years I was able to relate this immediate obedience to my walk with the Lord. As I grew up, the Lord kept before me the quiet purpose to prepare for His work in China. Since women doctors were needed to care for Chinese women, I worked toward a degree in medicine.

By the time I finished pre-medical studies at Washington State University in Pullman, Washington, the Great Depression of 1929 gripped the nation. There was no money to complete my medical training, so I took the necessary education courses and taught high school science for five years to earn money to go on to medical school. I found I liked teaching, but still had my eyes on the goal of becoming a doctor.

During those days of the depression, teachers' salaries were low. The school boards often did not have enough money to pay the teachers' salaries at the end of the month so we were paid with a promise to pay called a **warrant** instead of a check. If you could keep the warrant until it was **called**, and only then, you could receive its face value. Otherwise, if the money was needed for daily living expenses, it could be sold at a discount, that is, whatever you could get for it.

At last, with great effort, I was able to keep one warrant until it was called. That day after school, I went straight to the bank and deposited it – a full one hundred dollars. The next morning the bank did not open! I was shocked to learn that the biggest bank in our city had failed, and all my wealth of one hundred dollars was gone.

Of course I was disappointed, but I thought I understood how the brokers on Wall Street felt when their millions were gone, only I had the Lord, and I wondered how many of them did. I knew I belonged to Christ and that He would take care of me, and He did!

I began to fear I would be considered too old by the time I finished medical training, and would not be accepted on the mission field. It would take from eight to ten years more to complete my medical degree and to get the necessary Bible training. I knew a thorough background in Bible study is essential for a missionary, so after much prayer, I gave up the dream of becoming a doctor and went to Bible School at Prairie Bible Institute in Alberta, Canada. I graduated in April, 1936, was immediately accepted by China Inland Mission, and now, in October of the same year, I was in China.

I prayed, "Lord, here I am. Where do I go from here?"

Sleep finally came, and it seemed as if morning dawned almost immediately. I thought about my parents so far away in Mt. Vernon, Washington. Night was just falling there; my family would soon be going to bed, and here I was getting ready to start a new day. It was a comfort to know that the same God watched over us all and kept us united in His love, though we were far apart.

As I dressed for my first full day in Shanghai, I recalled one of the last talks I had with my parents before I sailed. I heard then, for the first time, that Mother and Father had dedicated me to the Lord for His service before I was born. I was glad they had not told me before. I had made my own choice with no pressure from anyone. I was so glad I had.

Then, as I began to rejoice because **I had chosen** to be a missionary, God gave me John 15:16 – **"You have not chosen me, but I have chosen you..."** I knew then that it was not my choice, but my obedience, that brought me to China!

I had always hoped to go to the people in Inland China. I wanted to learn their language so I could tell them, in words they understood, that Jesus loved them and paid the price for their sins.

Before I left home, some people had suggested that, since I had been a teacher, I might possibly be sent to the China Inland Mission School for missionary children in the city of Chefoo. I almost rebelled; I thought, "If Christian teachers are needed anywhere, they are surely needed in America." But the Lord showed me that missionary children are, indeed, an important mission field. They are not automatically saved because their parents are Christians. As with everyone else, each must make his own decision. The parents of those children were in Inland China doing the Lord's work. They were giving the gospel of Jesus Christ to those who did not know Him. This school solved the difficult problem of educating their children. Without the school, the parents would have to take time from their work to teach the children themselves or send them to their home countries. Before I left home I knew I would go to Chefoo School if that were God's choice.

During the few days we were in Shanghai, we were interviewed by the men who headed the Mission. These interviews helped them to get acquainted with us and to decide the best place of service for each new missionary.

In our free time we became somewhat acquainted with the city. We found we were entirely within the Foreign Concessions, far from the native city. Even so, there were many Chinese in and out of the place.

Traffic on the streets was much like that in Japan. Cars, busses, streetcars, bicycles, motorcycles, wheelbarrows, rickshas and all, each going according to the whim of the driver.

Very few horses were used to pull loads; men did that which was not done by women. Most of the horses I saw were mares led, covered with blankets, through the streets. If anyone wanted to buy milk, the mare was milked into the buyer's glass and the milk was sold – just like that.

To add to the confusion, Japanese invaders were causing trouble in the countryside. Scores of Chinese refugees were pouring into Shanghai with all their worldly goods packed around them in their rickshas. They were seeking protection from the foreign powers in Shanghai.

Because there was fighting in the northern provinces of Shensi, Shansi, and Kansu, all missionaries from those places had evacuated to Shanghai and other points south to safety. It could have been a frightening situation, but **perfect love casts out fear.** I knew I was in God's will in coming to China and I rested in Him.

CHAPTER 3

YANGCHOW
October 1936 – January 1937

After a few days in Shanghai, we were sent to language school in Yangchow. We were scheduled to spend six months there in concentrated study, learning to speak, read, and write Chinese.

"How wonderful!" I thought. "I will, after all, be sent to the Chinese in inland China."

As we started our language study each Chinese teacher gave his student a standard Chinese name which was then registered at the Consulate. I was **Fei Shuh Chen.**

I worked hard to get the right tones and inflections in the difficult Chinese language. My Chinese teacher was most patient. He said the same words over and over, and I repeated over and over trying to get his approval. It was extremely interesting and challenging. There were times when I wondered if I would ever be able to learn the words and tones of Chinese, but I knew that with God all things are possible. God would work out His purpose and enable me to grasp and use the new language. I enjoyed the study tremen-

Language school in Yangchow.

Some of our Chinese teachers. The one with the scarf was our writing teacher. The one to the far right was my oral class teacher, Mr. Fave.

dously in spite of Satan's attempt to discourage me.

Our daily schedule was carefully worked out and strictly enforced. A special time was set aside for study in addition to our class instruction. We were not allowed to study at any other time; we had to learn to keep a healthy balance between work and relaxation.

During our free time, we were allowed escorts to guide us around the city. Chinese employees of the school took us to visit the shops and to see the sights. Everything was quite different from anything we had seen at home.

We found Yangchow, with its half-million people, to be a very wicked city. There was a strong anti-foreign sentiment. Some of the people were friendly and called us "foreign teachers." Others, full of hatred and suspicion, called us "foreign devils." It was unwise for more than five or six of us to go out together, so we took turns going out, whether to church or sightseeing.

One afternoon, a friend and I, guided by a sweet little Chinese woman from the school staff, went to visit another mission compound. As we walked through the streets, quite a crowd of children and adults gathered and followed us shouting, "Foreign devils!" After all, **no one but a devil would have fair hair and blue eyes.**

How I longed to know the language so I might be able to speak to these people and tell them about the Savior who loves them. As I walked, I prayed that the love of Christ might be manifest to them, in some way, even though I could not speak a word they could understand.

Yangchow's landscape was beautiful. The tiny

Three bridges over the Yangchow Canal. This part of China is truly beautiful.

farms gave a patchwork effect to the countryside. A small piece of land was enough for a farmer to work in his primitive method using a water buffalo for the chief beast of burden. All other work fell to human hands and backs.

The fields were very dry. There had been no rain for weeks. The land under cultivation must be irrigated and each farmer had his own irrigation system.

One system, a kind of water wheel, had a thatched roof above a large wheel, which was perhaps five feet in diameter, with small buckets attached all around the rim. It was turned by a blindfolded water buffalo going round and round in a small circle. (The blindfold was meant to keep the animal from getting dizzy.) As the buffalo went round and round, the wheel turned and lifted water from the stream, or pond, below to the field above, and poured the water into a ditch which carried it into the field.

Another type worked on a similar principle. This one had two bars, one above the other. On the lower bar were several sets of pedals. The upper bar, which was three or four feet above the lower one, was straight. Men, sometimes women or children, held onto the upper bar with their hands and "bicycled" on the pedals below. In this way they lifted the water from the pond to the ditch.

These streams were not like the clear mountain streams with which I was familiar. They were used for everything from drinking water to scrub and wash water. That water was filthy looking – a dirty greenish-brown with a very unpleasant odor. It is no wonder the Chinese never drink plain water. They drink tea made from hot water and so did not suffer from all the diseases commonly carried in the water.

I was amazed at the thousands of mounds in the countryside and learned they were graves. The size of the mound indicated the importance, or wealth, of the person inside. Acres and acres of the best land was taken up by these graves. Many of a farmer's ancestors might be buried in the middle of his little farm, making that part unproductive. I was told later that every five hundred years the land is leveled and they start over, otherwise they would have no land left for farming.

There were also other types of graves. Some were made of sun-dried brick or stone. The casket was set on top of the ground and a stone grave, like a little house, was fitted closely around it. An opening about six or eight inches long and two or three inches wide, near the eaves of the roof, allowed the spirit of the dead to go in and out.

As we looked at those graves, we were reminded of the vast number of Chinese who had died without Christ and had never heard the gospel. How sad it will be for them at the resurrection when those in the graves come forth for judgment and eternal punishment.

My mind did not continue to dwell on those who were already dead. I thought of the millions yet living and perhaps on the brink of eternity who were **without hope and without God.** How I longed to be able to present the gospel to them so they need not go to Christless graves.

If you could have seen the dull, sin-deadened, hard faces all around us! Even in my first days in China, I felt that we were in the devil's territory where "**Satan's seat is**" and that we "**wrestle not against flesh and blood, but against principalities and powers, against spiritual wickedness in high places.**"

Night and morning the temple gongs added their slow, weird, "tin-panny" beat to the heathen atmosphere in an effort to get the attention of their gods who might be asleep and would not hear the prayers that were being offered to them. It reminded me of Elijah's contest with the priests of Baal in I Kings 18. I yearned for the ability to speak the Chinese language so I could tell them of the true God who neither slumbers nor sleeps.

One day a friend and I visited a Chinese market. How dirty everything was. The fruits and vegetables were probably good, but they were spread on the ground and not at all attractively displayed. The meat was out in the open and covered with flies. One could smell the fish for blocks. Our only safe purchase would have been live fish, cleaned and sliced while we watched.

Later, we went through a foreign section where the marketplace was clean and everything attractively displayed under glass. What a difference!

The streets in old Yangchow were rather strange. In some places they were not more than three feet wide. Any work that could not be done in the house was taken out into the street. When a ricksha or wheelbarrow came along, everyone squeezed tightly against the wall so it could go by.

Those narrow streets were also very crooked with sharp turns designed to confuse the demons so they could not get through. I thought they were enough to confuse anyone!

The Chinese say that China lies on the back of a great dragon. Lest the dragon be hindered as he turns over, the streets are made of cobblestones put down in such a way that the beast can turn over easily. Those stone streets were not easy to walk on, but at least the dragon was comfortable.

One day my language teacher, with many words and much acting, because I still had so little understanding of the language, told me the ancient Chinese idea of the moon changes. He said, "When it is the time of the dark of the moon, they say the white moon has been eaten by the dark moon. The people then beat on drums, and make all manner of noise, to frighten the dark moon away and call the white moon back. When it reappears, they say it was not eaten after all."

Another day as my friend, Mary, and I walked down a street in Yangchow, we heard a strange noise coming from a nearby fence. A box, a ten to fifteen inch cube similar to a bird cage, hung in the sunshine. We walked closer to investigate. Inside the box sat the biggest cricket I had ever seen. It must have been three inches long! We watched as it rubbed its wings together to make its tune, and wondered if it was performing especially for us. We would have stayed longer to enjoy the song of the cricket, but a policeman came by. From the tone of his words, (we could not understand what he said) we got the feeling it would be best to move on, so we did.

China had many beggars. It was really shocking to see some of them. It was hard to see people in such need and be absolutely unable to do anything to help them. If something was given to one beggar, there were immediately two or three dozen around, literally shouting, almost starting a riot, trying to get the same attention and gifts. We would have been happy to help them, but past experience had shown that anything that was done to help must be done in secret.

On our way to town one day, we saw a very pathetic little old woman sitting at the side of the street – begging. She was apparently a victim of leprosy but the disease was beyond the contagious stage. She had taken off one wee cloth shoe and was holding her tiny foot in a cold little hand trying to warm it. Her toes had been taken away by the disease. Her hands were deformed, and so was her face. One could only get a fleeting glance while passing, but it was a most pathetic picture.

Another beggar, an old man, blind and dressed in rags, was on his knees at the side of the street. Whenever he heard someone coming, he bowed to the ground and bumped his head on the pavement to get the attention of the passer-by.

In one store we saw a far stranger sight. A Buddhist priest stood a short distance ahead of us. He had his back toward me; I could not see his face. Near him, with a display tray slung over his shoulders, stood a poorly dressed man. On the tray was a jar of preservative solution containing something which, from that angle and distance, I could not identify. As we crossed the street to another store, the priest came, too. He appeared to be a fine, robust, young Chinese man. He was large, strong and healthy looking, but his left hand had been cut off at the wrist. He entered the store and asked the men working there for money. The little man who followed him displayed the jar and its contents – a human hand!

China had many poor people and many were beggars.

The priest had cut off his perfectly normal hand to show his devotion to Buddha. He was now spending his life begging – in the **service of his god**. I shall never forget that man and the picture it gave me of China's need. I wondered if he had ever heard the Good News of Jesus' love which I could not yet express.

It is not easy to present the gospel to one of those priests because of the language barrier and their hardness of heart. I prayed that someone might give him the gospel and that he might be saved.

When he asked alms of those men in the store, they all laughed and told him they could not give to him because they were Christians. They were not, but they had heard something of the gospel. Because of our presence, they were hiding behind us and using us as an excuse for not giving to the Buddhist.

My heart went out to those people to whom I could not yet speak, but I knew that God was able to make me fluent in their language. I could not express how happy I was to be in China, but the Lord knew. Whenever I thought of the way God had brought me to China, the soul-searching, the ocean voyage, and all, my heart was filled with joy and peace. I knew that China was where He wanted me to be.

We had not been long in Yangchow when I received a letter from CIM Headquarters in Shanghai asking me to prayerfully consider going to Chefoo School. I didn't **need** to pray about it, for the Lord had already prepared me. He seemed to say, **"That's it!"** and I knew that was exactly where He wanted me. **No more language school**

for me! The Lord was sending me to Chefoo School where I would be teaching in English.

CHAPTER 4

THE SCHOOL AT CHEFOO
JANUARY, 1937

I left Yangchow on January 15th by train and arrived in Shanghai the next day. After a week in Shanghai gathering warm clothing and things I would need for the colder climate in the north, I was on a ship bound for Chefoo.

Tension between the Japanese and Chinese continued to increase. At Wei-hai-wei all the Chinese passengers left the ship for fear of the Japanese. I was the only passenger remaining, and enjoyed being "Queen for a Day" for the rest of the trip – all the stewards were serving me.

When the ship arrived in Chefoo, several members of the school staff were waiting for me on the dock. We gathered my luggage and hurried on to the school. It was night and all was dark; so I could see little of the school. I was shown to my room in the large brick building that could house eighty to ninety girls and the staff members who were responsible for their care.

The next morning I was able to see the size and beauty of the school compound. I admired the

J. Hudson Taylor, the founder of CIM, planned the Chefoo School in 1879. In 1881 the boarding school for children of CIM's missionaries opened.

beautiful brick buildings and marveled at the growth of the school since its beginning in 1881. In 1879, after years in China, the founder of CIM (Hudson Taylor) had come to Chefoo in ill health. The sea air and good climate aided his recovery. While he was regaining his health, the Lord led him to plan a school here for the children of CIM's missionaries.

With a good boarding school here, the children would not have to be sent away to their parents' home countries for their education, which often meant they would be separated for years.

Mr. Taylor was able to buy some land near the beach at a reasonable price. The lumber from two wrecked ships, the Christian and the Ada, provided material for the first building.

In 1881, the school opened with one building, one teacher and three students.

Now, in 1937, there were ample facilities to house and care for 350 boys and girls and the school staff. There was the **Prep School** with a dormitory and classroom building for children six to nine years of age. The **Boys School** and **Girls School** provided separate dormitories for boys and girls from ten to eighteen years of age. Some of the unmarried members of the staff lived in each of the three dormitories and acted as "adopted" parents to the youngsters. The Boys and Girls Schools had gone co-educational by 1936, so now boys and girls had classes together in the new Co-ed Building. Separate houses or apartments were provided on the compound for married teachers and their families.

Each school had its own sickroom and nurse. A doctor and hospital on the compound provided

Chefoo Staff.

care for more seriously ill children and for ill or retired CIM personnel.

Chefoo School was established primarily for the education of CIM children whose parents were on the mission field in inland China. These families were mostly British and American but included some from other European countries. The children must be able to fit into the environment they would find when they returned to their home countries. So the curriculum followed the pattern of British schools, and classes were taught in English.

Children and teachers had little contact with the Chinese world outside the walls of the compound, though Chinese servants were employed. With 350 children to care for, servants were a necessity.

Children from other mission groups and those of foreign businessmen were accepted if there was room for them, and if they could handle the work and the English language.

Chefoo School gave the children a high quality education. Each year the Oxford College Entrance Examinations were given to those who were to graduate. All who passed the examinations were eligible to enter any college or university in the home land. There were very few failures.

Members of the administrative and teaching staff were mostly British. I was the only American at that time, and it was my responsibility to see that the American children met American educational standards.

There were three vacation periods each year — a two week vacation at Easter, three or four weeks in the summer, and a long vacation of eight weeks

Chefoo Staff for the girls' school.

My group of girls. The girls are wearing the school uniform.

in December and January when travel was safer from the health standpoint.

At each vacation one or more staff members escorted each group of children to a central city where the parents from that area met them and took them home for the allotted time. At the end of the holiday they regathered in the same central city, were met by the staff members and escorted back to school. Those children whose parents were in Yunnan Province had the longest trip of all – three weeks of travel to get to their parents, two weeks at home and three weeks to get back to school! China is a big country and travel at that time was very slow.

When I arrived on January 26, 1937, I was assigned a room in the Girls School and met the staff, as well as the children who had been unable to go home for Christmas and those who had just returned from the north. Two days later the group of about sixty children arrived from Yunnan and the southern provinces. Classes began on the 29th.

I soon found that missionary children are like all others. Some were mischievous, some naughty, some boisterous, some quiet, some happy, and some unhappy. I loved them all – sweet, lovable little rascals they were. They needed the love and discipline their parents should give, so we, the teachers and staff, provided it.

My duty, in addition to teaching, was to act as mother to a group of ten and eleven-year old girls. Each staff member was an acting parent to the students in her room or grade, loving them, teaching them, and bringing them up in the nurture and admonition of the Lord.

The parents were so far away they could not see the children often. The separation was hard for both parents and children. Some families were separated from one to three or four years at a time.

Most of the children understood why their parents were in China's interior and knew that their lives were in the Lord's hands. They felt the peace of God and were happy.

It isn't easy to learn to live and work with those of another culture and Satan soon began his attacks. Since I was the only American on the teaching staff, I sometimes bore the brunt of anti-American jokes from the British. I remembered that I had been warned before I arrived on the mission field of Satan's attacks on new missionaries. This was one of them, an attempt to destroy my relationship with my fellow-workers, to magnify differences and cause disharmony and incompatibility.

In times of difficulty, I remembered that **"God is able,"** and I learned to say with Paul, **"I can do all things through Christ who strengthens me."** (Philippians 4:13) There was, at times, a bit of nervous strain, but I liked the work, the staff, the children and the school.

The staff members were lovely Christians and fully qualified teachers. Most were British – from Great Britain, Canada, Australia and New Zealand. They did all they could to make me feel at home and to help me adjust to the British curriculum and grading system which was so different from that in the States. I had a full schedule and was teaching subject matter I had not studied since I was in grade school, as well as high school subjects.

During those years the American Navy summered at Chefoo. It was a beautiful sight to see the ships coming into the harbor in formation. Unfortunately, this was their last summer because of the deteriorating Japanese political situation.

The highlight in May, 1937, was the celebration at the British Consulate of the coronation of King George VI of England. The entire school was dismissed to enjoy the festivities of the occasion.

We were on our way by ricksha to the celebration, when I noticed that the streets in our compound had been freshly sanded and were slick. My ricksha-puller was quite human and wanted to show how well he could manage the rick on the slippery hillside street. I urged him to slow down and be careful, but he **knew he could handle the rick!** However, it took just one tiny moment to lose control. The rick flipped over and threw me out.

I got up, a bit shaken. The only damage we could find was a scraped elbow, so we went into the Girls School for a Band-aid, then on to enjoy the celebration. Two or three days later, however, I collapsed. I fainted in the school hallway, and was taken to the hospital in Chefoo.

I was quite upset at being put to bed, on the sidelines and unable to do my share of the work. Finally, I remembered the warnings I had been given about Satan's three areas of attack on new missionaries: (1) he attempts to undermine the worker's health and lay him aside; (2) he causes discouragement by making him doubt his call to the field or by lack of visible fruit; or (3) he stirs up strife, criticism, misunderstanding, or differences of opinion between workers. One's only resource is to stay in constant fellowship with the Savior and seek His guidance and wisdom.

I recognized my feelings as the work of Satan and accepted the injury as a time to rest and wait on the Lord. I realized I had received attacks in all three areas – all in less than one year. Satan uses the same methods over and over, but these testings, plus the tension of the invasion, provided more opportunities for God to show His faithfulness.

God makes no mistakes. He had given me a strong, healthy body and a definite call to China. Though I couldn't understand all that happened, I knew I could trust Him.

· P·A·R·T ·

2

IN THE WAR
BUT NOT OF IT

CHAPTER 5

FALL OF PEKING
1937

My condition did not improve and a few weeks later (in late June) I was sent to Peking University Medical College Hospital in Peking where I underwent many tests.

On the morning of July 7, I awakened with the tension and sounds of war in the air. Japan was officially invading China in her quest for more land. Peking, the northern capitol, was her first target.

The great city of Peking is surrounded by massive stone walls fifty to sixty feet high and about twenty feet thick to protect the city from invaders. (Two cars could easily be driven side by side on the top.) One would think nothing could penetrate those huge walls, but would they protect from airplanes and bombs?

War brings fear and terror. Thousands of terrified Chinese had poured into the city to take refuge behind the walls during the siege. The city gates were now tightly closed. No one could come in or go out.

We heard explosions as the Marco Polo Railroad Bridge just outside the walls was blown up. The Chinese were untrained and unprepared for modern war. Their only weapons were swords, staves, a few guns and bayonets. Of course they were no match for the Japanese with their modern war machinery.

The people, packed tightly within the great walls, cried out, "What can we do?" "We'll starve!" "How will the farmers get food into this place?"

We wondered what the Lord would do. We knew He was our refuge and would protect us, and He did.

The Japanese never bombed the city of Peking because they had financial interests there. The siege of Peking lasted only a few days. During that time, those courageous, enterprising Chinese farmers were up at the crack of dawn. They came to the city gates with their produce, sold everything quickly, and rushed home safely before the Japanese got off their beds. So those people inside the walls received enough food to sustain life.

That situation did not last long. After the city fell, it was a different story. The Japanese were in control of everything and they let us know it. It seemed they were everywhere and into everything at all times, early and late, both inside and outside the walls.

I learned at this time what the Lord meant when He said that we, as Christians, are "in the world but not of it," for now we were "in the war, but not of it." At that time, as much as they wanted to, the Japanese could not touch American or British citizens, for America and Great Britain were still neutral. This was only a local war involving the Chinese and Japanese!

The doctors finally diagnosed my problem as a "delayed concussion." The treatment? Lots of peace and quiet, bed rest, and no school in September. How could one find peace and quiet when Peking was under siege and the terrors of war were all around us?

The doctors considered sending me home to the States to recuperate. I rebelled inwardly at that for I knew that if I were sent home within the first year I would not be allowed to return to the mission field. I knew God had sent me to China, and He assured me that it was His choice that I stay, even though the doctors wanted to send me home. Before long, they agreed there had been sufficient improvement and I could stay.

Finally, I was discharged from the hospital and was ready to get back to school and the children. I waited at Pei Tai Ho, a resort near Peking, for a ship, the only way to get to Chefoo.

Because of the war, travel was quite dangerous. Each day we heard over the radio how the Japanese, with their mechanized units, made amazing advances through the country. The Chinese had no mechanized units and no trained army, only a warlord here and there with a few men, untrained as soldiers, armed with swords and clubs. They had no chance of victory and very little chance of survival.

As the Japanese army infiltrated new areas, their officers went up and down each street ordering the Chinese families to send out their men and boys to fight in the Japanese army. As insurance against desertion, the Japanese military authorities made it clear that a deserting Chinese soldier would not be pursued. Instead, his entire family would be wiped out. What a way to control the behavior of those conscripted, unwilling Chinese soldiers! They dared not desert.

We were concerned about Chefoo School. It was in an ideal location for the children. It would also be ideal for the Japanese and we knew they would soon want it and take it.

We felt we had the right and the duty to ask the Lord's protection for our children so that they should not suffer the terrors of war. They were there for the sake of the gospel as were their missionary parents who were stationed all over inland China.

One night a group of us in Pei Tai Ho who were especially concerned for the children in Chefoo held a night of prayer. I'll never forget the prayer of one elderly lady who had spent her life on the mission field. Her prayer that night was that God would set His horses and chariots of fire round about Chefoo as He had done in the days of Elisha.

(Elisha's servant was frightened when he saw they were surrounded by the Syrian army and cried out "Master, what shall we do?" Elisha calmly prayed, "Lord, open his eyes." The servant's eyes were opened and he saw the mountains full of horses and chariots of fire. There were more with them than with the Syrian army. 2 Kings 6:15-17)

That prayer struck me so forcefully! It never occurred to me to doubt that it would be answered. I knew it would be! The question in my mind was, "How is God going to answer that?" I soon found out.

On October 26th, I was back in Chefoo. God did keep the school and the children safe and untouched. There was fighting all around Chefoo, but the city itself was perfectly quiet and within Chefoo School God's peace reigned. School went on as usual.

CHAPTER 6

FALL OF CHEFOO
1938

New Year's Day, 1938, came and went. The next day, Sunday, we had such a heavy snowstorm that the little children from the Prep School could not get to church. The Lord had purposely provided that they should have their service alone in their own building. We felt the Lord had planned the circumstances, **for the snowfall stopped as soon as the service began.**

One of the missionaries spoke to them concerning the power of Satan and the danger of dealing with him.

Some of the little boys had been singing a song that had the same message as **"Jesus Savior Pilot Me."** The words began, **"Do you want a pilot? Bid him come on board."** Instead, they were singing. **"Do you want a pirate? Bid him come on board."** They did not realize it, but they were really singing to Satan, which explained much of their recent misbehavior.

I wondered if those little fellows were seeking a repeat of the excitement of February, 1935 when a boatload of seventy youngsters, their chaperons and the entire crew of their ship had been captured by pirates? One crew member had been killed and thrown overboard, others were injured and some locked up. Strangely enough, none of those children were harmed, though all were frightened. To those youngsters, by the grace of God, the pirates had been kind and considerate, though fierce and pitiless to the adults. After about a week the ship was located by search parties, the pirates were frightened away, and the ship with its precious cargo of unharmed children returned to Shanghai. That ordeal provided an opportunity for the children to see that their teachers lived the faith they taught.

In 1938 the children had no need to seek danger if that was what they wanted. Danger lay all around us, though our compound was still relatively safe. Japanese soldiers with guns and bayonets were all over the city of Chefoo. Who knew who or what might be waiting around the corner?

Rumors of all kinds floated around:

"There are bandits in the hills. They are coming down to work the city tonight."

"The Japanese have taken over the city."

"The police chief has left Chefoo."

"The police are going to loot the city tonight."

Finally, on February 3rd, the Japanese took over the city amid a great show of planes, gunboats, submarines, soldiers, and Japanese flags. The Chinese gave no resistance whatever, and the Japanese takeover was completed with no bloodshed. They called it a peaceful takeover, but it was wartime peace, full of tension and terror.

Day after day, truckloads of Japanese soldiers rumbled past our compound and out through the city gate. There was fighting on the other side of the hill; we could hear the noise.

It was enough to strike terror in the staunchest of hearts, but the Lord, in answer to our prayers, gave us the assurance that He was in control.

In Chefoo it was perfectly quiet, so quiet that the Japanese called the city "Little Heaven" because there was no fighting there. They even went so far as to say, "The reason is that there are so many praying people." Wasn't that a good testimony from the Japanese? They were thinking of the prayers of those of us who were right there in Chefoo. We knew of people around the world who were praying for our children's safety.

Chinese believers were praying, too. There had been a gospel work in Chefoo for many years. There were some Chinese there who had long known the Lord and were strong, stalwart believers. Others had just recently been born again.

These people were suffering great affliction under the Japanese for war brings suffering wherever it is. In spite of that, those Christians met daily to pray. There was curfew and they could not be on the streets after dark; it would mean certain death. So they met at noon.

Though they were suffering, their prayer was not for the defeat of Japan, nor of victory for themselves, but that God would send the gospel to Japan. Those Chinese Christians believed that when God said, "Pray for those who persecute you and despitefully use you," He meant it. (How often we forget to pray for **our** enemies!)

We had been under Japanese "protection" ever since they had invaded China. One is more comfortable without such protection as they gave. We were still in the war and surrounded by it, but were not yet of it. We were free to move about from place to place, but there were definite restrictions because of fighting in outlying districts. It was definitely dangerous to go far from our school compound.

Whenever I went about the city in a ricksha, whether visiting or shopping; it was my ricksha coolie's duty to wait to take me home. However, if a Japanese should come along and want the ricksha, off my coolie must go. He was given no choice and I would be stranded with no way to get home. So, for his protection and mine, I bought a Chinese-made American flag. The stripes were sewn on a machine and the stars were hand-embroidered. Because the United States was neutral, I could put that flag in the seat of the ricksha and the Japanese could not take it even if they wanted to. (This worked until the attack on Pearl Harbor. From then on, of course, the Japanese showed no respect for the American flag or for us.)

Battles were constantly going on around us and over us. There was never any real let-up. One night a gunboat in the harbor shelled our friends in the village about ten miles away. We felt the shock waves from the shells as they were fired, heard the scream of the shells overhead, and the loud noise of the explosions in the village. We could have been frightened, but we knew the Lord was our protection and we were at peace, though we were concerned for our Chinese friends who were under fire.

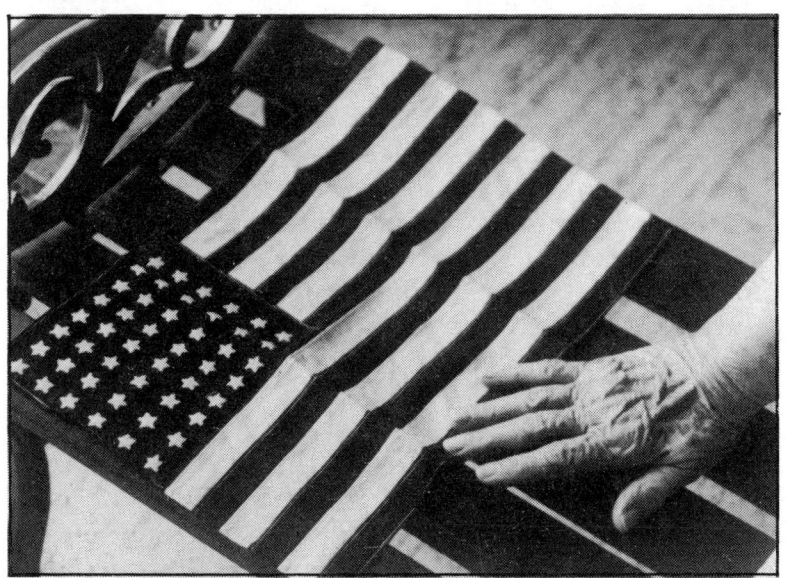

Chinese-made American flag (the stripes were sewn on a machine and the stars were hand-embroidered). I put the flag in the seat of the ricksha.

We watched the Japanese bring in their little seaplanes and load them with bombs in the sea just off our beach. We were terribly upset when the planes dropped those bombs on our friends' villages about fifteen miles away.

One day one of the Japanese pilots overshot the landing with his little plane and ended up on the beach – stuck in the sand. We could hear his Commanding Officer dressing him down. Of course, we stayed out of sight and chuckled. They had a hard time getting that little plane back into the water.

Night after night the Japanese probed the darkness of the hillsides with powerful searchlights. They were on the lookout for any Chinese guerrillas who might be trying to sneak into the city. One night they caught some Chinese trying to slip in disguised in sheepskins. Of course, they were quickly eliminated.

The Chinese made many attempts to stop the Japanese, but they had no chance of success against the mechanized units and superior equipment of the Japanese.

One night there was fighting right behind our compound where some Japanese were on sentry duty. Three groups of Chinese started coming down from the hills. There was one group coming down from Ning Hai Gate, one from Vineyard Hill and a third a little further over from the other side of Vineyard Hill. They planned to come down from these three different directions to surround and surprise the Japanese.

Our compound wall was rather low, only about five feet high at the end of the girls' dormitory. The street was just on the other side of our wall.

The destruction caused by air raids can be well imagined when we see this deep, gaping hole blown out of the solid earth.

I was on the sleeping porch on the second floor, at the end of the building nearest the wall. I could hear the men coming down from Ning Hai Gate clashing their swords together and shouting "KILL! KILL! KILL!" The other two groups were sneaking down silently to take the guards by surprise.

The Japanese sentries became nervous and called for reinforcements. The Chinese with no guns, only their swords and clubs, had no chance against the heavily armed Japanese. There was a real massacre just outside our wall.

When the bullets began to whistle past us too close for comfort, we got the girls out of their beds, for they were all on the second floor on the same level with the flying bullets. We went downstairs to the dining room and read to the girls while the fighting was going on.

They could not hear the fighting, so soon forgot about what was happening outside. Later, when the battle was over, we all went back upstairs and slept soundly for the rest of the night.

The next morning some of the girls told weird, gory stories about how they heard clean-up crews scraping up the remains. Their imaginations were running wild. Some of the bolder girls felt they must climb over the wall to see what had gone on. By that time there was nothing left to see for all the carnage had been removed.

In November 1938, because of the war, a group of young men, new missionaries for China Inland Mission, were sent to Chefoo, instead of the usual city of Anking, for their language study. (The young men and young ladies were never sent to the same city for language study.)

Before their arrival, one of the youngsters asked a teacher, "What will it be like when the men get here? Like the school for the prophets?" From that time on, that group of young men was called the **"Sons of the Prophets."**

When their ship arrived in Chefoo, these **Sons of the Prophets** had to be inspected by Japanese medical officers before they could leave the ship. The Japanese are small people and when the doctor and his assistant stepped into the room occupied by twenty-two young men who were each nearly six feet tall, they must have felt as if they were surrounded by giants. The two Japanese men took one look upward, gasped and stepped back in shock. Then both took a deep breath, as if to gather courage, and went forward to do their duty.

In a school of this size it was necessary to have sports events. The Sons of the Prophets took part in the athletic activities with the children, but they were always **handicapped** to make the competition fair. One youngster who wrote home about the sports events, said in his letter, "You know, 'So and So' is my favorite. He won the long run and he was **hanky-capped** too."

Throughout 1939 and 1940 the war situation became worse and worse. Japanese terrorism and oppression became heavier throughout Occupied China.

We did our best to keep school going on as usual, but soldiers and guards seemed to be in and out all the time, even bursting without reason into the classrooms. The noise of Japanese planes overhead was nerve-wracking. There were all kinds of water and air maneuvers around and over us adding to the nervous tension.

One day the Japanese surrounded the compound and took the Prep School's head cook away. They accused him of stealing money and gambling. When he returned, it was evident that he had been tortured. There were many such incidents that made the Chinese servants extremely fearful.

CHAPTER 7

THE RUSSIAN WORK
1939

There were many white (non-Communist) Russians in China who had escaped, with great danger to their lives, from Russia during the Communist "takeover." The Lord began a work among those Russians in Chefoo as the result of the prayers of some of our six-year-old children from the Prep School.

One day in the spring of 1939, my friend Linda, an Australian teacher, who was in charge of the small children at recreation time, took them walking along the beach. They met a Russian woman who was a very undesirable-looking character. With her was a little, white wooly dog.

Naturally, the children all wanted to pet the dog and Linda felt it would not hurt if she let them do so.

They played with the dog a few minutes, then started on along the beach. One little six-year-old asked, "Does that lady love the Lord Jesus?"

Linda answered, "I don't know. She doesn't know enough English to understand us. You children pray for her and some day she will."

The children began to pray for her every day in their group devotions and individually. One afternoon a little boy, who was coming home along the beach alone, saw the woman with her dog. He ran up to her and asked, "Do you love the Lord Jesus?"

"Course I do!" was her answer. (She didn't, that was just her answer to the child.)

"Then, why don't you come to our church?" he asked. "My daddy preaches over there sometimes."

A few days later, Linda was on the beach alone and met the woman again. This time the lady asked Linda, "May I come to your church?"

"Of course, you may. Come next Sunday," Linda told her.

Later, Linda told me what had happened. She asked, "Do you have any idea where we can get a Russian Bible or New Testament?"

I did, because the Lord had already provided it. Because I was the new teacher-missionary, I was shifted from room to room, occupying whatever room was vacant when its occupant was away. Finally, a senior missionary retired and I **inherited** her room. She left behind many old books. Members of the staff were to take those they wanted and throw the rest away. As I was clearing them out, I found a box with a lovely, leather-bound Russian New Testament. I thought, "Someday, someone will need this book." And I put it on my bookshelf.

I gave that Testament to Linda. She allowed the children to present it to the lady and it became her most cherished possession.

The lady and her German husband planned to

go to church with us the next Sunday. On Saturday, a measles epidemic broke out in the upper school exposing all the children ten years old and older. To prevent spread of the disease, they must now be isolated from the Prep School children.

We felt the Lord had a special purpose for that epidemic. For the next six weeks, services in Memorial Hall were geared to children six to nine years old. That was a great help to the Russian lady and her husband who knew so little English. They began coming regularly to these services.

Each Sunday as our guests came to the service, either Linda or I sat with them. When the Scripture was announced, we looked it up for her in her Testament, so she could read along in her own language while it was being read in English. (We could locate the portion of Scripture, even though we could not read Russian.)

Since Linda was free during class hours, Rena, the Russian lady, often came to her and they had Bible study together, either in Linda's room or on the beach.

One day when she and Linda sat on the beach studying, Rena said, "When I was a child, we studied the Bible in school. When the Communists came in, they said, **'That book is not true. Don't believe it. There is no God.'** So I just forgot all I ever knew."

But it was not beyond recall. As she and Linda read and studied in the Gospel of John one day, Rena said, "Once there was a man and he had some sheep. One of them got lost."

"Yes," said Linda. "You are that lost sheep and the Lord is not going to stop until He has found you."

Another day, as we were walking home from a Bible study, Linda spoke to me calling me "Martha."

Rena said, "There were two sisters, Mary and Martha. They had a brother named Lazarus. He died and Jesus brought him back to life."

One by one, the Bible stories came back to Rena. For months she and Linda studied and read the Scriptures together. One day they read in I John 5:11 **"...and this life is in His Son."**

"I want this life," said Rena. She found it that very day.

Some time after that we met a group of about eight or ten Russian-Chinese children. Their mothers were Russian, their fathers were Chinese. They were not accepted by either race. Their runny, infected ears indicated a desperate need for medical help. They had been to the priest of the Russian Orthodox church who had given them a very small amount of money and told them, "Now, don't come back!"

We tried to help in as many ways as we could. We asked our school doctor for help. He was very sympathetic, but he, himself, was not allowed to go to them. School rules prevented it because of the danger that he might bring back disease to the school children. But he gave us medicine and let us administer it. Soon the runny ears, colds, etc., were better.

Now that their physical needs were taken care of, we were able to begin taking care of their spiritual needs. We were able, though with a distinct language handicap, to start a Sunday School for those children and their mothers. We managed to get some Russian New Testaments, but we had no hymn books or chorus sheets, even though we had written letters trying to find a source of supply.

One must sing in Sunday School!

Later, when I took a journey into Manchuria, the Lord provided four Russian hymn books. The lady who was instrumental in getting them was a missionary friend who was serving the Lord in Dairen. She had a friend who was a Russian pastor. When she told him of our work among the Russian-Chinese in Chefoo and our search for much needed Russian hymn books, he said, "Perhaps I can help you."

He went home and came back with four hymn books – words only, no music. She had him hum the tunes of those hymns he knew. If the tune was familiar to her, she jotted down the English name beside the Russian title. We looked up the hymns in our English hymnals, fitted the Russian syllables to the music and learned to sing them. The Russian children and their mothers were delighted when they learned to sing in their own tongue. One song they really loved to sing was **"What can wash away my sin? Nothing but the blood of Jesus."**

At first, Rena would not go with us to this Sunday School. "They're low class. I'm high class!" she said. By this she meant they were poor and illiterate. But she would help us learn to pronounce the syllables phonetically, so we could teach the women to read. Oh, but they were glad to hear the Gospel in their own language!

By and by, Rena realized there were **no** classes before the Lord Jesus for we all need Him. From then on, she helped us. She went with us, read the Scripture, and taught the lesson in Russian.

Linda and I often went to Rena's home for Bible study. One evening we were met by a strange sight. Rena, her husband, and a Japanese gentleman in his silken kimono, sat at the table with their Bibles open before them.

Rena's husband called out, "Come on in! We're having good things here!"

In very broken English, the Japanese man said to us, "I hear God – call me – come – Chefoo – preach – my own people. They – not know – Jesus Christ."

Before he left Japan he had met a Christian Japanese student from Chefoo. The student had told him, "If you go to Chefoo, you must meet Mr. Herbert Taylor," (oldest son of Mr. Hudson Taylor, the founder of China Inland Mission) "and my friends, Mr. and Mrs. Klock" (Rena and her husband) "who live in the same apartment complex as my parents."

It happened one day that Mr. Herbert Taylor had dropped in on the Klocks for a visit and the Japanese man was present.

That evening we all sat at Rena's table. Each of us read from his own Bible – the Japanese man, in Japanese; Rena, in Russian; her husband, in German; Linda, an Australian, and I, an American, both read in English. We had no common language, yet we were able to have fellowship through the reading of God's Word. What a blessed, sweet time we had that evening. We all felt a thrill that transcends, or goes beyond language. God's Word bridged the gap.

In the weeks that followed, we became better acquainted with the Japanese man and his wife and often visited in their home. They had been in China such a short time that their furniture and supplies which had been shipped from Japan had not yet reached them because of wartime shipping conditions.

They were keen Christians who were very sad about what their country was doing in invading China, but of course they could do nothing about it.

One afternoon in April, 1940, we arrived at the home of our Japanese friends and found the house filled with a number of Japanese Christians who were having a prayer meeting. They continued to pray earnestly and undisturbed while someone went to get a bench for us. When they had finished praying, our pastor-friend turned to us and said in English, "You pray." We did.

It seemed he had made the "fatal" mistake of witnessing to some of the Japanese military personnel and had been ordered back home to Japan. That, and the fact that this group of believers was being left without a pastor, was the reason for the fervency of their prayers.

We never had any further contact with them. They were a precious couple, and we really missed having fellowship with them. We never knew whether they reached Japan safely, were "liquidated," or what happened to them.

The Sunday School for the Russian-Chinese children continued very effectively, with Rena's help, until after Pearl Harbor when the Japanese closed it down.

CHAPTER 8

PEACE IN THE FACE OF WAR
LATE 1941

By late 1941, the situation had become extremely tense. It looked so much like all-out war that our Mission Board sent word, saying "If any of you in Chefoo feel you should go home, you are free to go." Not one of us left in spite of the intense stress. We all felt a responsibility to remain at the post where the Lord had placed us and to take care of the children. If we had gone home, the parents would have had to come out of their places in the interior to take care of, and teach, their children. It was hard, but we gladly stayed.

The situation became more and more trying. Everyone carried on his work in as nearly a normal manner as possible, even though Japanese soldiers continually burst into our classrooms, as uninvited guests, interrupting our classes and generally making nuisances of themselves.

When vacation time came in December of 1941,

information was secretly given to the children that all who were leaving for the holiday should take all their possessions with them. We were facing the possibility of evacuation.

Because of the war, travel was extremely dangerous and slow. Distances were great, for China is a vast country. In those days, people traveled on foot, by ricksha, bicycle or wheelbarrow, by ship, bus or train. But now many of the railroads and ships were being bombed by the Japanese. There were very few cars, roads were little more than trails, and there was no air travel for civilians.

The first group of students was taken to Peking and Tientsin, where their parents met them. Those children got home to their parents, but never returned to us.

The next group, the southbound children, including those going to Yunnan Province, were all packed and ready to go on the same ship when it returned, but it never came back.

Perhaps one hundred children, or more, had gone to spend Christmas with their parents. We still had two hundred youngsters at the school. They could not get home. It was very disappointing to them and to their parents. The children comforted one another and settled in very calmly to stay on, for no one could do anything about it. Some of these children and their parents did not see each other for five more years.

On Monday, December 1, the beginning of Christmas vacation, the teachers and staff started a week of what our British friends called a **House Party**. We would call it a **Bible and Prayer Conference**. Those of us who were not on duty

The railroads and ships were being bombed, making travel dangerous and slow.

Donkey travel was a means of transportation for some. Pictured here is an evangelist and his burden-bearer.

with the children went to the home where the meetings were being held and stayed there together, night and day, concentrating on Bible study, prayer and fellowship. Those on duty with the children joined us during whatever free time they had.

We were not a group of backslidden missionaries, but I'm sure that some of you have found that it is easy to be so busy **doing** when you are serving the Lord, that you sometimes become slack on **being in His presence.** We were eager for a **fresh touch** from the Lord. Our burden of prayer was for revival — not a matter of a series of meetings, but a freshness of Life for ourselves.

On Sunday night, December 7, we studied and prayed and waited on the Lord. At about 1:00 A.M. He touched us and poured a spirit of praise upon us. We had a joyful time and watched until dawn.

Our study that night had been from 2 Chronicles, Chapter 20 — **Jehoshaphat set singers to praise and the Lord set ambushments and won the victory.** We had the assurance that He would do the same for us!

P·A·R·T 3

UNDER HOUSE ARREST

CHAPTER 9

UNDER HOUSE ARREST

Later that morning, as we sat eating a leisurely breakfast, the radio program was interrupted with a newscast that said, "The Japanese are at this moment bombing the American Naval Base at Pearl Harbor near Oahu, Hawaii."

We were stunned. We sat in silence, unable to move or speak!

Before we had time to recover from that shocking news, Japanese officers burst into the house and strode quickly into the dining room where we sat.

"You are all prisoners of the Japanese military. Everything in this school belongs to us, even that soap dish over there. We will be generous, we will lend you these things until we can find somewhere else to put you," they said.

They picked up our radio and left.

As the implications of this news sank into our minds we realized that America and Britain were no longer **in the war, but not of it.** We were no longer neutral. World War II had begun and we were all involved.

The Japanese soldiers took all the radios from the compound. The news of the attack on Pearl Harbor was the last direct radio news we had. From then on we knew little of what was actually happening.

All the **"foreign nationals"** in the area instantly became prisoners of war. Seventeen British and American businessmen and missionaries, including our school Headmaster, were jailed – accused of being foreign agents. The rest of us, including two hundred school children between the ages of six and nineteen, were placed under **house arrest**. We could only leave the compound with special permission and must wear identifying armbands.

We were placed under military control which was not a comfortable place to be. Later, we were transferred to the custody of the Consular Police – the Civil Authorities.

Our new commandant, who had his early training in a missionary school in Japan, understood something of our situation, and the reason for our being there. He did everything he could to make things easier for us. He was not a Christian, but he thought enough of his Bible to carry it with him to China in his limited wartime luggage. One day our school doctor asked him where he could find a Japanese Bible.

"I have one you may borrow, if you like," he said.

When the doctor started reading this Japanese Bible, he found the Japanese and Chinese characters to be identical, only the pronunciation was different. **He was able to read the Japanese Bible in Chinese.** (Since then some Japan-

We were placed under "house arrest" and had to wear identifying armbands.

ese characters have been changed and Chinese and Japanese Bibles are no longer interchangeable.)

Since we were now at war and I was the only American teacher in the school, I had to go all the way across the city of Chefoo to the American Consulate to get citizenship papers for the American children. Passports were not required for them as long as they stayed in China. That was quite a saving for us. Now that the United States was in the war, we must have citizenship papers for them in case we should be repatriated.

I also carried with me a complete inventory of the possessions of the American children and other American Mission members, including all the furniture, both school owned and personal. Everything had been claimed by the Japanese as their property.

I had a strange feeling as I walked across the city, for I was suddenly an enemy. I did not know what to expect.

The Consulate, a two-story brick building, stood on a street corner at the top of a hill. It was surrounded by a high iron fence with big iron gates on both sides of one corner. A burly Chinese soldier stood guard for the Japanese in front of the gate. He had not chosen to be there; it was that or lose his life.

The man looked to me as if he were six feet tall. (The northern Chinese are much taller than those from the south.) In his layers of quilted garments, he looked enormous, especially to me, because he was guarding the gate I had to go through.

In my very best Chinese, I said, "Please, may I go through that gate?"

This is a typical Chinese gate where the Japanese would force Chinese men to stand guard.

Very gruffly, he said, "NO!" and turned his back.

I quickly opened the gate and hurried in. Afterward, I was surprised that I had sense enough to read the man's signals. My natural reaction would have been to say, "Well, Lord, if You are not getting me in this way, what are You going to do? You know I have to get in."

The guard had done his duty. He had told me not to go in, then quickly turned his back so he would not see me do it. What chances some of the Chinese took in order to help us!

I hurried into the Consul's office. I talked with him and turned over the inventory of our possessions. The guard was not at the gate when I came out. Had he decided to guard the gate on the other side of the corner at that moment? The military police would never leave the Consulate gates unguarded.

Twice more I had to go to the Consulate. Both times the guard must have seen me coming and had gone around the corner to guard the other gate. I never met him there again.

As I crossed the city on the way home after that first visit to the Consulate, I happened to walk in front of the building where the seventeen men were being held prisoner. I saw Mr. Bruce, our Headmaster, looking out through a window. Until then we had no idea where they were.

On Christmas Day a strange thing happened. Those men were allowed to go home to their families for the day, but had to return to their prison the next day.

For forty-three very trying days, those seventeen men were held prisoner. Then, suddenly, for no human reason, all but one were released. That one, a Christian businessman, was retained. He later died in the hands of the Japanese.

After the men were released, they told us that no one could ever know what it meant to them to see me walk past in such a perfectly normal manner. They realized then that all the stories they had been told by their captors about what had happened to us at the school were false, and they were encouraged.

Those men, non-Christian as well as Christian, said that their release was in answer to prayer. We all knew it was. Prisoners of war are not released until the end of the war unless there is an exchange. From the human standpoint, there was no reason for it. The Japanese just let them go. Again, we could see God at work answering our prayers and protecting our people.

One of the seventeen prisoners was a medical doctor with another Mission whose children had been in our school. He had sent his wife and children home to the States for safety before the Japanese struck Pearl Harbor and the war began. One day after their release, we invited him to have dinner with us at the Girls' School. In the course of the conversation, he told us that a few years before, a member of his mission's national board had come to visit. That man told them how he made it a practice to read the Bible through twice a year. It was such a blessing to him that he recommended it to his mission.

The doctor went on to say, "I thought, 'That's alright for you. That's your business; you're a preacher. But I'm a busy doctor with a hospital. I couldn't possibly do it!' But I did and it was a

85

real blessing. So I'm recommending it to you teachers on the Girls' School staff."

I thought, "That is interesting, but doctors have office hours and some free time. We teachers at the Girls' School are responsible for eighty-seven girls twenty-four hours a day. How could we ever do that?"

But I tried it, and for several years I read through my Bible two or three times each year. **It was a real blessing.**

C·H·A·P·T·E·R

10

FINANCIAL PROBLEMS
1941 – 1942

Shortly before the incident at Pearl Harbor our school treasurer had received a check with which to buy food and supplies for the holidays. On Saturday, December 6, he had taken that check to the bank to be cashed. (All the banks had been Japanese controlled since 1938 when they took that part of China.) At the bank he was told, "We can't give you the money today. Come again on Monday and you may have it."

They knew exactly when those first shots would be fired. If they kept that money until Monday, it would be theirs – and it was. We received not one cent from that check which was to pay for the children's needs.

What could we do with two hundred children to care for and not one penny coming? We prayed, "Lord, they are Your children. We are just looking after them for You."

Then we prayerfully considered the situation. What would the Lord have us to do? We counted our pennies. There is never much money on the mission field. If there had been much, it would have been put in the bank for safekeeping and would have been taken by the Japanese – as were all foreign accounts!

We started by putting ourselves on a very strict ration, as strict as we dared, for one thing we must do was to keep the children healthy. We did not want them to suffer for the rest of their lives because of improper diet. We substituted foods we had not formerly used, but which were equally nutritious, for those familiar ones we could no longer get. Everything was rationed including bread, milk and eggs. Each child knew how many slices of bread he could have each day. If anyone ate more than his share at breakfast, he was hungry before night. We were never really hungry, but we never had a satisfied, full feeling when we left the table.

We found that by very carefully maintaining those strict rations, we could feed the children for three months – but then what? We had already seen enough of the war to know it could not be over in that time. We also knew the Lord would supply the need in answer to our prayers – but how?

I hope you have had the experience of receiving a definite answer to a definite prayer. If you have not, I urge you to pray definitely. God answers just as definitely as we pray. He wants to answer our prayers. He gives us that assurance in John 15:7 saying, "If ye abide in me, and my words abide in you, ye shall ask what ye will, and it shall be done unto you."

One day, before the three months expired, our secretary was working in his office when a Chinese businessman came in. The man was very upset.

He said, "I am in a place of great distress. I have this money (it was a large sum) which I must get into Free China immediately, and the Japanese won't let it out of Chefoo. Can you help me?"

He knew nothing of our needs. He was concerned with his own needs. He must pay his bills or lose his business. He had to keep his business going to keep his family fed.

We had been cut off from the rest of the world since Pearl Harbor. No mail could come in or go out, but our secretary was able to send a message **"over the back fence."** It was relayed by Christian friends until it reached Mission Headquarters in Chungking, far away in Free China, that part of China the Japanese had not yet taken.

(CIM Headquarters were originally in Shanghai. As the war clouds grew darker and more ominous, the Lord had led Mission leaders to send a **skeleton** staff, duplicate records and some funds to Chungking in Free China. Immediately after Pearl Harbor all **enemy nationals** in Occupied China were prisoners of war and the CIM headquarters in Shanghai was closed. Our skeleton staff in Chungking took over and we were never without CIM Headquarters in China. From then on support money was sent to Chungking instead of to Shanghai. How glad we were for the Lord's leading.)

There was money in the treasury in Chungking for us, but if it were sent to us, it would be taken by the Japanese. The Mission Treasurer in Chungking used our money to pay that man's bill and we used his money that the Japanese would not let out of Chefoo to meet the needs of the children. It was an even exchange, and both his needs and ours were met.

We told the children about the money – the answer to their prayers and ours. That night they held a praise service to thank God for sending the money.

When I went through the hall a few minutes after the service was over, an excited eleven-year-old girl came up to me and exclaimed, "Isn't it wonderful? God has answered two prayers and He is going to answer the third!"

"What prayers have been answered?" I asked.

"Oh! They released our Headmaster and the other men; and God sent us the money we needed."

"And what is the third?" I asked.

"God is going to let us get letters from our Mommies and Daddies."

That doesn't usually happen in wartime, but it did this time. The children were allowed to send and receive no more than one letter a month. Sometimes even that one did not get through. Can you imagine what it meant to their mothers and fathers far away in the remote areas of China to hear from their children, and what it meant to the children to hear from their parents? What a precious answer to prayer!

Every time we began to run a little short of funds, (we never got to the point where we could see the "bottom of the barrel") another businessman would come to our secretary with the same request the first one had made. The same man never came twice. We did not know the men's names, nor did we want to know. That was a safety factor. If one should have been **"caught,"** what might he have revealed under torture? We were never "caught."

At the end of the winter our medical staff reported that this had been the most healthful winter in the record of the school. The children had not been out to be exposed to measles, whooping cough and chicken pox. Neither had they had as many cases of colds and flu as usual. The Lord had blessed our substituted foods and met all our needs.

Since our funds were short, we dismissed some of the servants. In our situation servants were a necessity to meet the needs of the children and to keep the school going. There was cooking, dishwashing, cleaning, laundry, mending and such to be done.

We did not have the convenience of modern appliances. Clothes were washed by hand on washboards and ironed with old-fashioned sad-irons heated on the stove.

(I once taught a Chinese amah, a serving woman, to test the heat of the iron by dampening her finger and touching it to the bottom of the iron. One day as I passed by, I saw her stand back and spit at the stove hoping to hit the iron. I don't know about the iron, but the stove sizzled, and she did not burn her finger!)

We adults began to take time from our teaching and other duties to do work we had not had time to do before. The boys and girls learned to accept responsibility and did things to help with the housework, such as setting tables, washing dishes and doing some of the cleaning.

There had never been any need to boil our drinking water. We were blessed with an artesian well on the compound that provided all the clear,

Water carrier in Chefoo, China, 1940.

pure water we could use, but it was not piped to the buildings. Water had to be carried in large containers to the places where it was needed.

When the Japanese took over, they said, "That is not your well. It belongs to everybody!"

"Everybody" began to come and use our water and before long the well was contaminated. From then on, we had to boil our drinking water. However, we were thankful we still had water, even though it was no longer clean and pure.

The Japanese officials began going from house to house, family to family, of all the **enemy nationals** in Chefoo asking, "How much money have you?"

Some told the truth and some did not, but if they lived too long on what they said they had, there was trouble.

Our whole mission group was considered one family by the Japanese. We knew we would tell the truth if they asked us about our money. We also knew we would live too long on the amount we had on hand because the Lord would supply more.

"Lord, don't let them ask us that question," we prayed.

They never did. They often came to the secretary with a long list of questions. They would reach the point that the next question would surely be, "How much money have you?" and for no apparent reason, they would go into some other line of questioning. Not once did they ask about our money!

The Japanese never did discover that secretary and treasurer are often the same. To them, the secretary only took notes; the treasurer handled money. Our treasurer's official title was "Secretary." They never suspected him of being our treasurer and handling the money.

One day in March, two masked Chinese men with guns burst in on our secretary as he worked at his desk.

"Your money or your life!" they demanded.

"No indeed!" said the secretary.

"I'll fire," one of the Chinese threatened.

"Then, fire. Go ahead, fire!"

The man fired – at the ceiling. Then both Chinese men fled from the building with nothing.

The Japanese placed no value on the lives of the Chinese, and since all our cooks were Chinese, Japanese guards began going to the kitchen demanding food. Our frightened cooks, in order to save their own lives, gave it to them.

One day a Japanese guard came in, held out his helmet, and demanded: "I want this full of sugar." It was given to him, even though our supply was short and sugar could be bought only at black market prices.

One night our supply of ham and bacon was stolen from the cupboard where it had been stored. Padlocks were then put on all the storage places to prevent such raids in the future.

Our food was disappearing right off the compound. How were we to feed the children with our supplies running away like this? We were desperate. What could we do? Could we report them? We were prisoners. What rights have prisoners?

We were God's prisoners, so we had **"Throne Rights."** No one could stop us from going to the Throne of God in prayer. So we prayed about the problem.

Then our men took some legal paper and made a very beautiful, very ornate document with dotted lines in the center and an official-looking seal at the bottom. The next time the guards approached the kitchen, two or three men from the staff went through the main entrance, down the stairway, and met them at the kitchen door.

The Japanese politely stepped forward with their demand.

With politeness almost exceeding that of the Japanese, our men came forward.

"Why, certainly! We'll be delighted to give it to you. Just sign on the dotted line and write down what you got."

They quit coming. They knew they were doing wrong. They were afraid we'd report them and they would be in deep trouble. Of course, if we had reported them we would have been in deep trouble with them.

The biggest problem confronting us continued to be that of providing sufficient food and a balanced diet for two hundred children. But we were still confident that God would continue to answer our prayers and meet our needs.

There were many tests along the way. It seemed that Satan was having his day, but the Lord was at work keeping His children safe. We were constantly under pressure, but through it all the Lord gave us peace and the assurance that we were His prisoners. We knew that God was in charge even though the Japanese thought they were. Adults and children alike rested in God and were filled with His peace.

C·H·A·P·T·E·R

WHAT IS GOD DOING?

For eleven months the Japanese kept us in constant turmoil. Every few days they came with a different order – "Next week we will move you to (and they would name a certain place)" and the next week they would order us to move in another direction, from a cold area to a warm one and vice-versa.

Our two hundred children, the teachers and staff were kept busy packing and unpacking every week or ten days, preparing each time to go to a different location, but never going.

One day the officials came and said, "We're going to put you in those buildings over there."

"Those buildings over there" were an old hotel on the waterfront that had been condemned as unfit for human use five or six years before. Shortly after Pearl Harbor the Japanese army had occupied those buildings – and how they occupied them!

(The winters are extremely cold in Chefoo – so cold that the water in the inner harbor froze over a few years before this and the ships could not

96

come in. People went out on solid salt-ice in rickshas to meet the passengers in the outer harbor. **The weather must be very cold to cause salt water to freeze.**)

The Japanese soldiers in that building were cold. They put on their wadded garments for warmth. They put on more and more clothes and looked broader and broader, but were still cold.

They chopped up the furniture and burned it to warm themselves. They were still cold, so they took up and burned the floor, board by board. When they left there were no floors, no furniture, no windows or window facings, no doors or door facings, no lights or light fixtures. There was nothing but a shell of a building.

Did they really intend to put two hundred school children and the school staff in that place?

We said nothing to the Japanese authorities. We went aside and prayed, "Lord, don't let them put us in any place that will not be for Your Glory and for the good of these children."

The next day the officers were back saying, "So sorry! We can't let you have those buildings. The navy wants them."

They thought **they** had changed their minds. They didn't know it was the Lord's doing.

The army and navy both wanted our property. Neither would give in to the other. For eleven months we had the use of our buildings while they argued. When they finally took complete control, a brick wall was erected right down the middle of the compound. The army took one side and the navy took the other.

The time came, at last, when the Japanese military took over our Business Department and tore down that building. They held an idolatrous prayer service on our hillside asking their gods to bless their building.

"Lord," we asked, "how can You allow these heathen to come and destroy Your Heritage?" We could not understand what was happening; we knew God had a purpose and He would let the Japanese go only so far.

They prepared to erect a brick building there for the stables, and built the forms for the concrete foundation. When they went home that night, everything was ready for the cement to be poured the next day. Then it began to rain. All night the rain came down and their carefully built forms were filled full of mud!

The next morning when we saw the havoc done by the rain, we just stood back out of their sight and laughed. **The Japanese had asked their gods for a blessing, and our God had filled their foundation up with mud!** They had to dig it all out again.

Finally, one day the Japanese authorities came with the demand, "You must close the school. We want this building and that building."

They were taking our two new fireproof buildings – the classroom building for the older boys and girls, and the Prep School building for the six-to-nine year old children. Up until this time we had continued all classes as usual. Now our school was closed and we were crowded into the remaining buildings.

We watched the Japanese carry away our precious textbooks and library books, which could never be replaced, in burlap sacks to be used as waste paper. We never knew what they did with our school furniture.

We could not have two hundred children with nothing to do now that the school was closed, so we started a week of special Bible and prayer services for them and a week for ourselves. Again, the burden of our prayer was revival – a fresh touch for our hearts and theirs.

Our meetings were suddenly cut off in the middle of the week with an order to go to Temple Hill – a mile or more away from the beach, on the opposite side of Chefoo, where we would no longer be able to see what the Japanese were doing on our beach.

We began to wonder, "Have we been praying wisely? Does it pay to pray for revival? The situation seems to get worse each time we pray for revival."

When we first prayed for a fresh touch, America was drawn into the war. This time we were ordered into concentration camp as prisoners.

We soon realized that before God could lift us up as we desired, He must first bring us down to the point of knowing that we were absolutely helpless and dependent on Him. Then He was there to meet our needs. Yes, we had revival!

P·A·R·T 4
INTERNED!

C·H·A·P·T·E·R

TEMPLE HILL
November 1942 – August 1943

"YOU MUST BE OUT BY FRIDAY. IF YOU ARE NOT OUT, THERE ARE ENOUGH JAPANESE SOLDIERS TO PUT YOU OUT." Those were the orders we received on Tuesday, November 3, 1942. For eleven months we had been under house arrest in our own mission compound. The Japanese had been constantly trying to move us, but in every instance they had changed the orders. Now we had definite, immediate orders to move to Temple Hill on the opposite side of Chefoo, away from the beach. From there we would no longer see what the Japanese were doing on the seashore.

There were three mission compounds on Temple Hill which had been owned by the American Presbyterian Mission. Like our Chefoo School compound, this property had been taken by the Japanese when Pearl Harbor was bombed. The Presbyterian missionaries had been interned in some other site and the buildings had been vacant for eleven months. The Japanese had already interned about one hundred people, (missionaries and business people) in the two houses of one compound and part of one house in the second.

Three and one-half houses were waiting for our two hundred children, the school staff and a number of retired or ill missionaries (British, American, Scandinavian, etc.). Well over three hundred people were to live in three and one-half houses.

We had all been prisoners for eleven months, and school activities had been going on much as usual, except for unexpected, unscheduled visits from guards.

The children dreaded the change and crowded space as much as the adults did. Being prisoner in your own room with your own things around is very different from a concentration camp with almost nothing of your own and with so many people crowded into so little living space. However, we all knew we were there at the Lord's bidding and God was still in control.

By the next day, Wednesday, the children's boxes had been packed exactly as we had been ordered, then loaded on hand-pushed carts. The children and some of the staff lined up and formed what the children called a **crocodile**. In their arms they carried anything they were allowed to take but could not get into the boxes. They marched across the city, singing and praising God with their favorite choruses.

The one they loved best of all was:
"God is still on the throne,
He will remember His own.
His promise is true,
He will not forget you."

It was a triumphal procession, not a sorrowful bunch of prisoners marching into a concentration camp.

As the children marched through the streets, every Japanese guard they met stopped them, inspected their things and took anything he wanted. It was **public looting in the name of the law.**

As the youngsters came near Temple Hill, they saw high stone walls surrounded by barbed wire entanglements – pieces of barbed wire were strewn about to snare the feet of anyone who ventured into the vicinity.

The huge gates swung open, the children marched in, and the gates slammed shut. Bare stone walls ten to twelve feet high and fifteen to eighteen inches thick met their eyes. The tops of those walls had pieces of broken glass embedded in the masonry to prevent anyone from climbing over.

Everywhere the children looked, armed guards were snapping orders. The arrogant attitude of those officers showed that they felt they were in total control. They did not reckon with the control **our Heavenly Father** exerted over them.

In spite of the disorder and tension in the place, the parents and teachers felt God's peace in their hearts. Because the adults were calm, the children were too. Every one knew the Lord was still in control.

"It is too late today to move your things inside," the English speaking Japanese guards told the children. "Just stack your boxes out here by the side of the house. You can take them inside tomorrow morning."

That evening, after the guards had gone away for the night, men from the school staff went around the compound and checked the gates. Every padlock on the gates had been removed and the bolts well greased, so the Japanese could slip in silently during the night. It was evident they intended to take the rest of the few things the youngsters had been allowed to keep.

Our men had some padlocks of their own for which the Japanese had no keys. They put one of those locks on each gate and the children's things were safe.

The next day, Thursday, the rest of us from Chefoo Compound made our way by ricksha across the city to Temple Hill. I had been assigned to stay with this group and to help them. There was one lady over eighty years old, a few retired missionaries, others in poor health, and two mothers with very young children, none of whom were able to do much work. There were forty-seven people in this group assigned to an eight-room house. (We used six rooms for sleeping, two for cooking and eating.)

The Japanese are very fond of children, but two hundred were too many at one time. They were very glad for us to take charge of them. We, in turn, were grateful that the Lord had arranged for us to have that privilege. When that news reached the parents, they too, were thankful that the children were still in our care.

Since the Japanese officials did not want the responsibility, we were allowed to organize the details of our daily routine – **even to continuing our schoolwork.** The children's education must not be neglected!

In our house we selected two teams who worked on alternate days to plan, prepare and serve meals — I was in charge of one team. We allowed a few teen-age girls to help in the kitchen.

We had plenty of problems. We had barely enough cooking and serving utensils for we had brought only a few of those things with us. There was no usable cooking stove in our house, just an old broken-down wood-burning stove that did not work.

For the first few days we cooked on two Primus stoves we had brought along. The little Primus stove was more like a burner to be used in a chemistry lab than something to cook on. It was tall and narrow — about twelve inches high with one little burner about four inches in diameter. There was a kerosene tank underneath and, like a Coleman stove, air had to be pumped in to get the fuel to the burner. It was quite a trick to balance a large pot of porridge for forty-seven people on that tiny burner.

We ate our first breakfast in silence — silence so thick you could have **cut it with a knife**. Each of us was thinking, "Why? Why has God allowed all this?"

For eleven months He had kept us in our own compound with everything seeming to go our way. Now, here we were in Temple Hill with everything apparently against us. What did it all mean?

Suddenly, from across the high stone wall, we heard a brass band playing "Standing on the Promises of God." What a message that was to us! God's promises are just as sure when everything seems against us as when it is for us.

But who could be playing that hymn? We finally learned it was a band from a Chinese mission school that had been taken over by the

Japanese. Those Chinese boys were being trained to fight in the Japanese army. Every day they marched to that tune. To Christians, it gave great assurance; to unbelievers, it was a good marching tune and nothing more.

Finally, the boys did learn one other tune. We thought there was a message behind that one. One line of that tune said, **"Massa's in the cold, cold ground."** That was undoubtedly their wish for their Japanese captors.

"STANDING ON THE PROMISES OF GOD!" We felt anew the assurance that God was with us and we continued to tackle the problems that faced us.

In just a few days, the men had the broken stove working. In a few more days, they had built a brick stove to use in addition to the old wood-burning stove. That was a great help in preparing the meals. One big disadvantage was that we had to buy wood for both stoves and then fight all day to keep the fires going. But it was nice to have two usable stoves!

There was also the matter of sleeping accommodations. We had not been allowed to bring our beds, only thin cotton pukais, (more like heavy quilts than mattresses) to be put on the floor to sleep on. When we were packing our bedding on the hand-pushed carts to leave Chefoo School, I put my bed frame and good innerspring mattress on top of the other things on the cart. Everything would be inspected and I **knew** the bed would be taken off since it was in full view. We were amazed when it was allowed to go through.

When we put our pukais in our tiny upstairs room, which was not much bigger than a walk-in closet, I gave my good bed to an **old lady** who was fifty years old. We four **young teachers** slept on the floor while the old lady had the bed. I could not have enjoyed sleeping on the bed when that lady was so much older than I.

That lady snored every night, so loudly that the **shingles rattled.** In the morning she would stretch and say, "I did not sleep a wink all night." The rest of us wished she would try sleeping if she made that much noise while she was awake.

It was a bit difficult to get up and down to make up those beds on the floor. There was barely room to walk between the pukais. It was good exercise, but it soon got monotonous. The monotony continually grew worse through the weeks, months and years until the end of the war.

That sleeping arrangement wasn't too bad as long as the weather was cold. We were so crowded that, with all the body heat, it did not take much fuel to keep the rooms warm. When summer came it was different. The heat in our tiny room became unbearable, so two of us moved our pukais to the tiny lean-to-garage attached to the house and spread them out on boxes and trunks to make a level surface. It was less stuffy there where the temperature only went to 116 degrees each day!

We were moved to Temple Hill in early November. Thanksgiving Day was only two or three weeks away. We wanted our British friends to understand and participate in our American Thanksgiving celebration, so we made the day as special as we could.

One of the American ladies told the story of the first American Thanksgiving – the whole story of the Pilgrims and their Indian guests. We prepared the best typical Thanksgiving dinner we could — using substituted foods.

We could not get turkey, so we cooked some chickens we had fattened. A native Chinese berry was substituted for cranberry sauce. We ordered pumpkins for pie. Day after day we ordered pumpkins and they did not come. I had heard about, but never tasted, sweet potato pie. I would try almost anything once, so at the last minute we decided to try making sweet potato pie. The pies were delicious even though we didn't know how to make them. The pumpkins came the next day — too late!

The day was a great success, enjoyed by everyone — in spite of the substituted foods.

Soon after Thanksgiving, we made plans for a Christmas celebration. We decided to make as many gifts as possible for the youngsters. The boys made baskets to decorate the tables.

A few days before Christmas we **built** a Christmas tree with nails, wires and pieces of evergreen branches. The children enjoyed helping to decorate the "tree" with paper chains and whatever else we found or made to hang on it.

We were awakened at 6:00 o'clock on Christmas morning by carols played on the Victrola (record player). That day we were allowed to visit, under police escort, in the other two compounds. Brothers and sisters, who had not seen each other since early November when we had come to Temple Hill, were extremely happy to be reunited — if only for a few minutes. Everybody greeted everybody else as long lost friends while the police escort waited impatiently to return us to our quarters.

From this time on we were allowed, if we made written application two weeks in advance, to visit friends in the other compounds for a few minutes, under police escort, and at their convenience.

We could not neglect the education of the children. In January, after we were settled, we started classwork once more. All the teachers kept their classes going under crowded conditions, with no desks and barely enough supplies to meet the needs. The science class was severely handicapped by the lack of equipment, but we managed to teach the scientific facts.

Since I was the only teacher who knew shorthand, I taught that class. My boys and girls sat on pukais on the floor – their knees in the air, shorthand notebooks on their knees – to take dictation. (They learned in spite of the handicap, for years later in Toronto, I met one of the girls who had been in that shorthand class. She told me that when she got home to Toronto after five years internment, she went to a business school and took a test to see what courses she would need in order to get a job. Her skill was great enough, she was told, that she did not need anything more, just to go out and apply for a job. It had been at least three years since she had received shorthand instruction in the concentration camp, for I was on the American exchange of prisoners, and she, a Canadian, was not.)

When the war was over, the Oxford College Entrance Examinations were given to these youngsters by the Oxford Committee. There was not one failure among them, even after five years of war.

The Lord had blessed our effort to continue the

education of the children in spite of the difficult circumstances.

A German-Jewish dentist and his family, who somehow had escaped from Hitler's regime and persecution, had settled in Chefoo a short time before the bombing of Pearl Harbor. Ralph, their ten year old son, had been accepted into Chefoo School where he was very happy. For the first time in his life, Ralph was accepted as a human being. The stigma of being born a Jew was lifted.

Now we were on the inside of the camp at Temple Hill and Ralph and his family were on the outside. Since Germany and Japan were allies, they were not interned with us.

One day, Ralph's mother stood outside the stone wall at Temple Hill talking to the Headmaster.

"If the Japanese would allow it," she asked, "would you be willing to take Ralph into the concentration camp and into the school with the other children so that he might be with his friends? This is the first time he has ever had friends, and now they have been taken away from him."

To Ralph and his parents, it was better to be inside a concentration camp with friends than to be outside without them. Of course, the Japanese did not permit it. We know nothing more of what happened to Ralph and his family.

CHAPTER 13

ADJUSTING

From the beginning, even before we left Chefoo School, our Japanese captors required us to line up in the yard each morning and evening for roll call. We had to learn to count off in Japanese. It is amazing how quickly one can learn to count in Japanese when one must. Other than that and a certain amount of Japanese intrusion, we were allowed to continue to plan our own activities.

We could not have two hundred children with nothing to do in their free time. So we continued as many as we could of the sports activities we formerly had for them at our Chefoo School compound. Other than sports, the girls had the Girl Guides Organization, similar to our American Girl Scouts. We organized Boy Scout troops for the boys (they all took part) but the projects they could undertake in concentration camp were limited.

My work in the kitchen was often interrupted by one or more of the scouts coming in to ask, "What is this plant I've found?" or "Come and see this new bug I've found! What is it?"

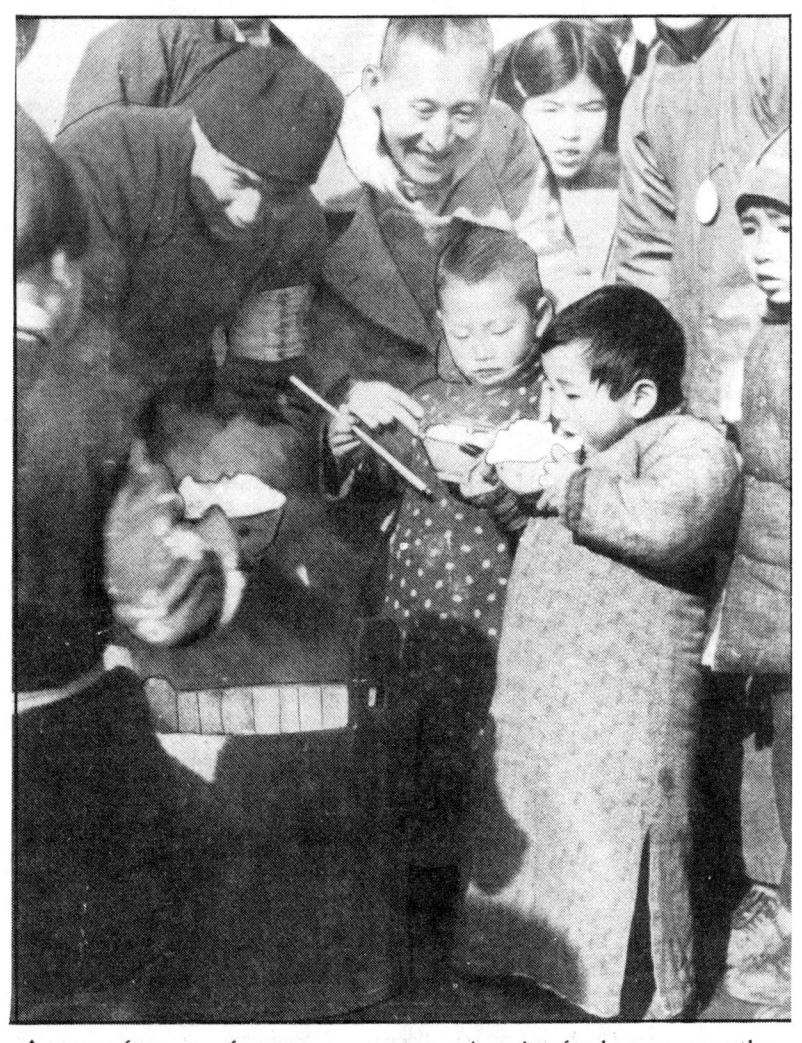
A scene from a refugee camp — steaming rice for hungry mouths.

Some of the teen-age boys expressed a desire to work in the kitchen because we **did such interesting things**. So after the first of the year, we allowed two boys **and** two girls to help in our kitchen each day.

The kitchen work counted as a scout project. The boys learned to build and control cooking fires in the wood-burning stoves and ovens. They learned to prepare food for the table, to plan meals and to order foods for the large number of people in each house.

They learned many of the basics of first aid — how to clean and bandage a wound, to take care of simple injuries and when to get help from an adult. They learned to work together in harmony as a group. Those scouts were quite helpful in many ways around the compound.

Our diet suffered from shortages of many things, especially fruits, vegetables and other foods rich in calcium for building strong teeth and bones. We relieved the calcium shortage by drying egg shells and pulverizing them. Each child was given a spoonful every so often. Later on, we had a little more variety in our foods.

We had never had butter or margarine in the summer as we had no refrigeration. We had always made and used a great deal of peanut butter. Now that we were interned we had fewer peanuts and no longer had our large peanut mill. We could make barely enough peanut butter to get by, not the generous amounts we had always used before.

Occasionally, we had another new product — milk made from soybeans. This soybean milk was not at all palatable to our tastes. Tofu, a bean curd made from soybean milk, was readily available. It was similar to cottage cheese made from cows' milk. The soybean curd was heated over a smoky wood fire which gave it a smoky flavor. One had to develop a taste for it, but it supplied necessary nutrients as tofu is a good source of protein.

We did the best we could to make the meals interesting for everyone, but we were all still hungry. The children did not always like the food they were served, but they were hungry enough to eat it anyway.

There was one lady in our house who was a diabetic. Of course, she should not have foods made with sugar. Whenever we made cookies for the children, we always made some special ones with saccharin for her. She ate her cookies and then asked for **her share** of the others.

While we were prisoners in our own compound, we had paid for our own food. The Mission Board could not send money directly to us; but, as you already have read, the Lord supplied funds.

As required by International Law, the Japanese government now began to allow a limited amount of money per day for their prisoners' food and fuel expenses.

"You had better be careful how you use this," they said, "for we will not increase the allowance this winter. You'll need to buy coal for heat, too."

So we planned the meals very carefully. We did our best to serve a balanced diet with the necessary foods, vitamins and minerals. We saved all the money we could so we could buy fuel to heat the buildings during the winter.

We had never been allowed to do our own

shopping, while under Japanese protection, either at Chefoo School or at Temple Hill. The Commandant sent a man to take our orders and go to market for us. We ordered what we wanted, (like the pumpkins for Thanksgiving dinner) but were thankful for whatever we got. The kinds of food we had before were not always available, so we often had to accept substitutes. The man always brought us something whether it was what we ordered or not. It was usually two or three days after the food was delivered before we knew its cost. Each man who had anything to do with handling the food had to receive a percentage of the cost (the Chinese called it a **squeeze**) to line his own pocket.

The Americans were more accustomed to eating a variety of foods than were the British. We educated them to eat and like cornbread. They had **never** eaten anything like **that**. To them, corn was animal food, fit only for cows and pigs. We were always able to get cornmeal, so we had cornbread or cornmeal porridge (mush) often, and the British learned to eat it with us.

When the Japanese first took over, they asked the men on our staff whether they would prefer to have rice or wheat. The men chose wheat which they sent to a mill and had made into flour. The flour was of poor quality, but we could make bread which we baked in the brick ovens our ingenious men had built for us. The wheat allowed us to have more variety in our diets than rice would have.

(Our white bread in China was so dark! One day on the streets of Chefoo, I saw a hand-pushed cart loaded with bags of flour. The brand stamped on the bags was **GOOD EARTH**. I thought there must be a lot of good earth in that flour to make such dark bread!)

Our meat in that camp had long ears, but it wasn't rabbit, it was donkey. Donkey meat is tough, coarse and stringy. If it is cooked long enough and seasoned highly enough, it can be made quite palatable. Most of our meat was made into ground meat which is easier to chew and can be cooked in a greater variety of ways.

One day while grinding donkey meat, my finger went too far into the grinder. I received a bad cut – almost to the bone. I was taken to the hospital in Temple Hill under Japanese escort. The injury was examined and sewed up. The finger was very painful for several days, but the Lord was good, and I was soon back to full activity.

There was a millstone about six feet in diameter in the basement of our house. (The upper stone was rolled around on top of the lower stone to crush the grain.) It was built to be turned with donkey power, but we had no donkey, and no way to get one into the basement if we had owned one. If we could manage to turn the millstone enough with our own power, we could have cracked wheat porridge for Sunday breakfast. That was a real treat!

Our menus sounded good, but the quantity was small and the quality was very poor. No one ever had enough to eat. We were always slightly hungry.

There were always some kitchen scraps, so we decided to buy some chickens, fatten them on scraps and add chicken to our menu. The birds were brought to our house with their feet tied together, taken down to the basement and left overnight — still tied.

The next morning while I was cooking breakfast, I heard the basement door open and close again and again. We investigated and found that the boys from next door had gone down and were untying the chickens' feet.

Chinese chickens are very wild. When the boys untied their feet, the birds began to run, squawk and cackle. They flew about in every direction. In no time at all, they were out of the basement and scattered all over the compound. Of course the boys went after them. We couldn't afford to lose those chickens.

The wall at the back of our camp was only about five feet high on the inside because the ground sloped upward. On the outside, the top of the wall was level with the ground.

The Japanese officials had said earlier, "If anyone goes over the wall, he will be shot."

The chickens went over the wall and so did the boys. They caught every chicken and no boys or chickens were shot for the guards were not yet on duty!

By the time everyone got back, each chicken had a name. One was named for the Swiss Representative, Mr. Egger. Another was Phidippides (for the famous Greek runner) for they had to run hardest to catch that one.

By this time the boys considered all those chickens to be **friends**. We couldn't butcher those hens; they were all pets. So we kept them and fed them. (We did butcher most of the roosters.)

Chinese chickens are mostly skin and bones with a few feathers attached. They are just so skinny! The Chinese never feed them; they just let them scratch for their food. We wanted to eat those chickens, so we fattened them with kitchen scraps.

Then one day, one hen made an awful mistake. She laid an egg! No one would kill a hen that would lay a fresh egg. The eggs we bought were far from fresh. They were of very poor quality for no one had refrigeration to keep them fresh. Our hens were getting enough to eat, so others soon began to lay eggs, also.

We took turns – all 47 of us – in alphabetical order, having a fresh egg for breakfast. The rest of us ate the other kind. Of course, the privileged person who had a fresh egg could have it cooked any way he liked, so long as the process wasn't too complicated.

We had those chickens and we bought some more. After we had been getting eggs for quite a while, one hen decided she wanted a family. We selected fifteen eggs and put them under her. The children were thrilled to see how that hen snuggled down over those eggs. For three weeks she sat patiently, turning the eggs once a day with her beak. She left the nest only long enough to find a little food and water to sustain herself. The children soon found that the hen knew how to deal a lusty peck to anyone who dared meddle with her eggs.

During that three weeks, the children became very excited over the prospect of seeing chicks hatched. That was a new experience for them.

The teacher in charge of the Prep School came by one day. "When the chicks begin to hatch, will you let the little folks come by and watch them come out of the shells?" she asked.

Of course we would be glad to, so when the chicks began to hatch, we lined a basket with cotton, put in some eggs and baby chicks, and notified her. The little children, and even older folks, lined up and marched up the front steps of the house and walked by looking at the eggs and new chicks. They all had to **STOP, LOOK AND LISTEN**. (Our fifteen eggs produced fifteen chicks, an unusually good hatch.)

We decided to keep our baby chicks in a little house with walls of chicken wire that had been left by the missionary children who had lived in the house before. The morning the chicks were hatching, one youngster was out under a tree gazing at the empty house. He was apparently seeing, in his mind's eye, the baby chicks already in it.

Some time later, when the chicks were big enough to run about the yard, a cat came over the wall and killed one of them. After that experience, the children would gladly have killed every cat in China.

After the excitement of seeing our chicks hatched, people in the other two houses in our compound decided to get into the chicken business, too. Soon there were several clucking hens and their chicks wandering around the compound. They thrived on food scraps, bits of grass, seeds and bugs.

We found that another project our Boy Scouts could participate in was poultry raising. They learned from books what they **should do** to raise poultry. Then they learned what they **could do** in a concentration camp. Each boy took charge of the chickens for a certain number of days. I signed a number of certificates documenting the ability of those Boy Scouts to raise poultry.

Later, when the Japanese were ready to move us from Temple Hill to Weihsien, there were a goodly number of chicks not quite big enough to be eaten. The children were not going to leave them to the Japanese, so, in the dark of the night, they handed them over the wall to Chinese friends.

C·H·A·P·T·E·R

MORE GLIMPSES OF CAMP LIFE

We missed the abundant supply of good, clean well water we once had in our old compound at Chefoo School. Here at Temple Hill we had a shallow well, but there was never enough water for all the people in our house. It was only occasionally possible to pump a little water into the storage tank upstairs.

These were American style houses. Each had an inside bathroom with a tub and toilet. It was impossible to keep that one toilet clean, flushing and in good condition with forty-seven people using it and water so scarce.

We had to buy our water. It was brought in by Chinese coolies, on hand-pushed carts or on poles across their shoulders. The bath water came in five-gallon cans, already heated, ready for baths. A blanket-like cover was put over each can to keep the water hot.

When anyone was ready for his bath, he was given a two inch cube to put in the tub. When the water came to the top of the cube, that person had his share of the hot water. The rest must be left for the next person. We each had a bath once a week. What a luxury! Of course, we had a schedule as to who bathed on which day and how long he was allowed to stay **submerged** in the tub.

One extremely cold night in January, one of our men teachers stopped by the guardhouse gate. (We were allowed to walk around inside the compound as far as the gate house.)

The gatekeeper, a new policeman at the gate, said to Mr. B., "It's very cold tonight, isn't it?"

"Yes," said Mr. B. "It is very cold."

"It's **very** cold tonight," repeated the guard.

"Yes, it is," replied Mr. B.

"It's VERY cold."

The teacher agreed again.

"It's too cold for me to stay here. If you will unlock the gate in the morning and let me in, I'll let you keep the key overnight and I'll go home and sleep where it's warm," suggested the guard.

So Mr. B. took the key, locked the gate when the guard went out and unlocked it again in the morning when he came back. We were not worried, neither were we trying to break away and escape. We could be trusted. But that guard was not seen again at that post.

Many funny things like that happened. They were very serious but at the same time were amusing. On the other hand, there were many tense and difficult situations; but the Lord was always there making them bearable for us. A good laugh often broke the tension. I'm so glad the Lord gives us a sense of humor.

God has not said we will not have difficult times, but that **"when thou passest through the**

waters, I will be with thee..." (Isa. 43:2). We had rough times, but God was always there keeping His promises.

One day in March, the Japanese came in and demanded all the children's bicycles. Of course the children hated to give up their bikes. They had been gifts from their parents or grandparents. But, being well disciplined youngsters, they gave them up without complaint. They never saw the bikes again. I suppose those Japanese soldiers wanted to be **mounted police.**

You often hear of prisoners of war being beaten and mistreated by their captors. The only one of our people who was ever struck by a Japanese guard was a Eurasian woman (British and Chinese). She had lived in her own home just across the street from our Chefoo School compound and was imprisoned with us at Temple Hill.

One day her Chinese cook – a real country bumpkin, an odd looking fellow – came to see her. He had had his picture taken and came to show it to her over the low part of the wall, since he was not allowed to come inside. He was so proud of that picture!

Just as he handed the picture across the wall to the lady, a Japanese plain-clothes policeman slipped up behind him and grabbed it. That meant he was under arrest. The poor man was terrified.

The Japanese officer, with the picture in his hand, started off down the street and the poor frightened Chinese was supposed to follow. He did until he came to an alley he could run down, and he disappeared. He seemed to have evaporated into thin air! The police could not find him anywhere, so they came back, arrested the lady and took her to court!

They tried to make her tell them where the man had gone. Of course, she did not know where he went. She was something of a comedienne, and was showing how it happened. She demonstrated how the policeman had grabbed the picture and how the servant had reacted. It was really funny! One of the guards in the courtroom laughed. Another, to keep himself from laughing, struck her with a cane. She was not injured, just humiliated. Thus, while covering up their own amusement, the Japanese showed their disrespect for her. She was the only one of our people who was ever struck by a Japanese guard.

The Japanese fondness for children also caused complications. One day in the spring of 1943, a Japanese guard with swollen jaws came on duty in the compound where the girls were housed. He assured everyone there was nothing wrong with him; he just had a swollen face. He picked up one of the little girls, the daughter of a Chinese-Belgian couple, and played with her. He even let her finish his cigarette. **There was nothing wrong with him**, but two weeks later, the little girl came down with the mumps, and the whole girls' compound was exposed.

There were at least sixty-five or seventy girls sleeping on pukais on the floor of the attic of the one and one-half story bungalow. They were so crowded that there was no way to isolate any who were ill. The best that could be done was to place the pukai of any girl who came down with mumps nearer the window and move the others as far away as possible, which was not far. The mumps epidemic was still going on when we left Temple

Hill in August.

We had plenty of hardships, but we tend to forget them. We were the Lord's prisoners and were resting in His peace. We saw God constantly at work on our behalf. His works are what we choose to remember.

We often think of captors as treating their prisoners with cruelty. On the other hand, prisoners often hate their captors and treat them spitefully. We treated ours like human beings. We did not flatter or kow-tow to them. They did their duty. We sometimes felt they were harsher than they needed to be, but the way we treated them made a difference in the way they treated us. I know the Lord used that to make the whole situation easier. God kept many things from taking place that would have caused the situation to be much worse for us.

Many times the Japanese told us they were going to do a certain thing. We prayed about it and they came back later saying, "No, we can't do that, we'll do this."

They thought they had changed their own minds. They did not know that God was still on the Throne and still answering prayer.

C·H·A·P·T·E·R

15

A CONSECRATION CAMP

Before we were moved to Temple Hill we had special prayer meetings on Saturday night to deal with personal matters that one would not bring up before the whole crowd. We asked one another, "What will we do without the prayer meetings? We need that prayer time more than ever. Where can we find a quiet, private place for prayer? All the available rooms are already in use."

We searched until we found one place that was not being used for anything, the goat shed, and we had no goats. We cleaned that up, and it became our prayer room. We now held prayer meetings twice a week, on Wednesday and Saturday nights, for we sorely needed the Lord's guidance moment by moment.

One of the teen-agers who was helping in the kitchen was a boy about sixteen years old. (We'll call him John to protect his identity.) John had become downhearted and miserable. He was a Christian, but we have all seen some downhearted Christians. They bring no glory to the Lord or anyone else.

One Saturday night we adults had been down in the goat shed praying for various ones, including John. When we came back to the house from the prayer meeting, one of the other teen-agers came running up, quite excited.

"John's been converted tonight!" he exclaimed.

And John had been literally turned around (which is the real meaning of **converted**). No longer downhearted and miserable, John was radiant. Who knows what his controversy with the Lord had been? But he had reached the point where he agreed with the Lord, and his burden was gone.

Up until now, John had been a shy boy. It was a real trial for him to talk with even one or two people, but now he wanted to tell everybody in camp what the Lord had done for him. That, in itself, was a tremendous victory.

We were allowed to have Sunday services if we gave the Japanese authorities a complete outline of the message two weeks in advance. As we made those outlines, we prayed that the Japanese who read them might come to know the Lord. There should be some Japanese in heaven who were saved, or started thinking about the Lord and salvation after reading those outlines.

I had been asked to give the message for the next day, Sunday. As required, I had prepared the outline and sent it to the authorities two weeks before. Our doctor was to conduct the preliminaries. We had prayer with John and his friend who had reported his conversion before we went in to the service.

"If there is anybody who wants to give his testimony, let him do so," I told the doctor. "I don't care if I don't get to say a word." I didn't get to say anything. I had done my part when I sent in the outline.

John got up and thanked God in a beautiful way for putting him in a concentration camp because there he got to know the Lord as he never would have otherwise. Then, one by one, other youngsters got up and thanked God for specific lessons He had taught them in camp.

Then another boy got to his feet – his composure completely broken. "Last night," he said, "I went to bed early. Then I felt God telling me to get up and pray. I got up and began to pray for one thing, then another. Then, suddenly, I knew that God wanted me to pray for John. This is the first I've known of the answer to my prayer."

Even while he was praying, God was answering his prayer. We were constantly seeing immediate, definite answers to definite prayer. God delights to answer definitely when we pray definitely.

In our house there was one little fellow, less than five years old, who could not say **concentration** camp. He tried so often to say it and always finished up by saying **con-se-cration** camp. He knew more about **consecration** than he did about **concentration**. That is just what our camp became – a consecration camp.

Each morning and evening we had **house devotions**. The whole family – all who lived in each house – got together for Bible reading and prayer. In addition, each child and adult had his own private Bible reading and prayer time. Many of the young people, during this time, heard the Lord's call to serve Him in various parts of the world where they are serving Him today.

As soon as anyone had something new from the Lord, he shared it with friends. We truly had times of rich fellowship in the things of the Lord.

There were no great meetings to stir up emotion. A concentration camp is not an emotional affair; it is stern, hard reality from beginning to end. But, one by one, our boys and girls met the Lord as they had their own daily devotions, their own Bible reading and prayer. They met Him in such a definite way that their lives were changed. They did not have to tell us; we could see it. Of course, we were glad when they did tell us.

We had continually prayed for revival. Do you think we had it? We did, but remember, God's way up to richer spiritual experience is first down to a greater helplessness and dependence on Him. Every time we prayed for revival, God shut us up a little tighter until we could do nothing, and then He was there at work. As long as we could defend ourselves and take care of the situation, He let us do so. But when we were completely helpless and wholly submitted to Him, He took over and worked for our good. Everybody had something fresh from the Lord. Yes, we had revival.

Up until this time our children had not grumbled, but now they began to murmur, "We haven't anyone else we can help." I think that grumble was pleasing to the ears of the Lord.

And so He soon moved us – using Japanese hands, of course. In August, the Japanese moved us to the camp in Weihsien and crowded us into much smaller space. And they put into their own pockets the money we had saved for fuel for the coming winter.

C·H·A·P·T·E·R

GOD SENDS US TO WEIHSIEN
AUGUST, 1943

All the internees in the general area of Chefoo were being moved to the larger camp at Weihsien. We were to go in two groups or contingents.

I was in the first contingent, which was largely American, to leave Temple Hill. Each contingent included some from each of the houses on all three compounds.

One girl, who had been constantly exposed to the mumps since the beginning of the outbreak, came down with the disease the day before we were to start for Weihsien. There was one other girl in this group who had not yet had the ailment.

"Please, let the girl with mumps wait and come with the next contingent so the boys and others who have not had the disease will not be exposed," we asked.

They wouldn't even consider it. "No, she has to go with you," was their reply.

So we put surgical nose masks on the two girls to try to prevent the disease from spreading. Since I had already had the mumps, I looked after them and a girl who had hepatitis.

The first leg of our trip to Weihsien was by coastal steamer, a trip that should have taken only one day. Before we left Temple Hill, we had baked some cookies for the children to eat to supplement the salted raw fish and vegetables they would be served by the Japanese.

We got onto the steamer and a "young" typhoon struck. We stayed on the ship in the harbor for two days waiting for the storm to pass. The cookies were fast disappearing.

Finally, we pulled out into the jaws of the storm. The wind and waves had the ship rolling. One by one, the children began to get seasick. I looked about and there they were – lined up along the rail. About noon, one of the boys who had been hanging over the rail, as sick as he could be, came to me.

"Miss Philips," he said, "could I have some bread and peanut butter?"

By this time I was slightly seasick myself. I said, "You know where it is. Go and help yourself."

When the storm was over and things had calmed down, I asked him, "Joe, why did you want that bread and peanut butter when you were so sick?"

He grinned and answered, "I had lost everything I had, and I wanted something more to lose."

That was a rugged trip with so many (between 90 and 100 of us) packed into the hold of that ship.

Finally, we arrived at Tsingtao. We got off the ship and onto a train, then traveled two or three hours by rail to get to the Weihsien camp.

When we arrived, we found more than 1700 British and American civilians, missionaries and businessmen, already interned there. Among them were a number of young fellows who had left home years before to get away from that "miserable, religious influence." If they had seen a Christian on the streets of Peking or Tientsin, they would have crossed the street rather than to meet him. How far would they have gone to avoid a missionary?

But now they were all in distress and difficulty. All were behind stone walls and barbed wire entanglements. They were beginning to find that Christians had, not **something,** but **Someone** Who made a difference. We know of a number of them who found the Lord during the time of internment. Who knows how many more there might be? The Lord does not permit suffering for nothing!

Here we were crowded into miserable quarters, much worse than anything we had ever been subjected to before.

This camp had once been the American Presbyterian Mission College. Everything that could be removed from the buildings had been taken away. The few foreign style houses which had been left more or less intact had been taken over by Japanese officials. All that was left for us were small student shacks which had been stripped and now were nothing but bare walls and dirt floors.

The facilities for caring for our bodily needs were quite primitive – almost entirely lacking. We had only cold water for bathing. We just washed ourselves the best we could with a **"cat lick"** – a wash cloth and a tiny amount of water in a wash basin. Our toilet facilities consisted of a hole in the ground with some planks over it. We stood on those planks and hoped we would not slip and fall in. There was a feeble excuse for a wall around the men's and ladies' facilities which were some distance apart. It was a horrible experience for people who had been accustomed to America's modern conveniences.

The sick girls and I, along with a few others, were crowded into one of those tiny shacks. Our pukais on the floor filled most of the space.

The authorities in Chefoo had told us that everything was furnished for us at this camp, so we had brought only a little of our cooking equipment, a few odds and ends of dishes and tableware and almost no bedding. We were quite shocked and dismayed when we found there was nothing provided for us. I don't know what we would have done had not the prisoners who were already there shared their things with us. Some of them had no dishes and were eating out of sardine cans and the like.

We sent a message back to the commandant to notify those in the next party to bring everything they could, because nothing was furnished. What would it have been like if the rest of the prisoners from Chefoo (300 or 400 more) had come without blankets or dishes?

With the arrival of the second contingent, all the Chefoo prisoners were reunited in one section of the camp. By now the total number of internees must have reached 2400 or 2500.

Among our people from the China Inland Mission was Mr. Herbert Taylor, the oldest son of Hudson Taylor (founder of China Inland Mission).

Mr. Taylor was well over eighty years of age, a frail man and very stooped. When he got off the train at Weihsien, he straightened himself like a little soldier, and in he marched – a real Christian warrior marching into the Japanese camp. One had to admire the spirit of the man. (He and his younger brother, also past 80, met in England after his release, at the end of the war.)

Eric Liddel, the famous Olympic runner, who was portrayed in the movie **"Chariots of Fire,"** was also interned at Weihsien. During the months that followed, he was a great inspiration to the young people. (He died in the camp just before the war ended.)

During the time we were interned, we lost one youngster – and that was because he was a typical teen-ager.

It was impossible to buy leather shoes to fit everyone, so all summer we allowed the boys and girls to go barefoot in order to save their shoes for cold winter.

One warm morning when everyone came out for roll call the ground was damp from a heavy dew. The children, as usual, were barefoot.

Seeing a wire hanging down, one teen-age boy challenged another, "I'll bet you can't catch that wire!"

"I'll bet I can," replied the other. What teen-ager would not respond thus to such a challenge?

He jumped and caught the wire. It was a live wire. He was instantly electrocuted. The wire was not purposely there; it was a tragic accident. Of our two hundred children, that boy was the only one we lost.

There were three kitchens in the camp, each

preparing meals for 700, or more, people. The food was far from what it should have been. Very often it was spoiled, or spoiling, when it was brought in to the kitchens. The food situation was very difficult to cope with, but the cooks did the best they could with what they had to work with.

Chefoo was in the fruit producing section of China. Early missionaries had brought in seeds of all our common fruits: apples, peaches, cherries, pears and berries. Before the war we had been able to buy an abundance of fruit in Chefoo. Now neither the quantity nor quality of fruit to which we were accustomed was available. Until now there had been no fruit at all in the Weihsien camp.

One day shortly after our arrival a shipment of apples came, one box for each kitchen. One bushel of apples for 700 or more people! What could be done to stretch one bushel of apples far enough to give some to each person?

Those in charge of our kitchen knew we had brought a little sugar. They asked, "Would you ladies from Chefoo please make some apple pies?"

We baked pies on everything that would hold pie – pie tins, cake pans, cookie sheets, lids, and so on. Each of those who ate from our kitchen had a tiny taste of apple pie. I don't know what the other kitchens did, but they did not have pie and were quite envious of those of us who did!

At Weihsien no firewood or coal was available for fuel. The Chinese there burned grass, leaves, sticks, anything they could find. None of that was available to us. We were confined behind stone walls and could not go out. The Japanese brought in **coal dust** which could be mixed with mud and dried in the sun so it would burn.

Many internees were given the task of mixing mud and coal dust and shaping it into **coal balls**. Those coal balls had to be made up and dried in the summer in order to be ready to burn in the winter. What a messy, filthy job it was getting into that mudhole to stir up water and earth and mix it with coal dust!

We had been in Weihsien only a short while, perhaps two or three weeks, I lost track of time, when one day a list of names was posted. Those whose names were on that list were to go home on an exchange of prisoners. There was no possibility of appeal or exchanging places. One could not stay behind if his name was on the list, or go if it was not. If that had been possible, some of us might have felt there were others who needed to go home more than we did. As usual, we found that the Lord knew what He was doing and He was still in control. If those in frail health had tried to go, they would not have survived, for **the trip home was the hardest of all.**

This was an American exchange. Those children who went home had to plant their feet on American soil though their parents were still in China. Only twenty-five of our 200 youngsters were included. The others were British, Canadian, Australian, New Zealanders, etc., so they stayed on in Weihsien.

A British exchange was to take place the next year, but it never did. The Japanese demanded the return of five Japanese for each Britisher released. The order was so unreasonable that Britain rejected it. No nation would have accepted such an unfair demand. (We were exchanged on a reasonable one-to-one basis.) The rest of the prisoners were held at Weihsien until the end of the war three years after we were repatriated.

In 1945, when our American leaders heard that the Japanese were planning to "liquidate" the camp, they sent in American paratroopers to rescue those who were still interned there. Among the rescuers was a graduate of Chefoo School who came to help his old teachers. What a thrilling experience for all!

For centuries the Japanese had worshipped their Emperor as god. When Japan was defeated, their god, the Emperor, was defeated and they had nothing left to worship. General Douglas MacArthur sent a message to the United States saying, "Send us all the missionaries you can."

Almost no one was willing or ready to go. War had taught Americans to hate the Japanese. Two or three generations of Japanese, who should have been reached for the Lord, were lost. During those wasted years, a number of militant religions sprang up in Japan, and the people were no longer eager to listen to the gospel. There is a strong missionary work going on in Japan now, but at that time, the number of missionaries going there was "too little and too late."

P·A·R·T 5
GOING HOME!

C·H·A·P·T·E·R

OUR TRIP TO SHANGHAI
1943

Of our 25 American children from Chefoo, I was fully responsible for seven older girls and shared responsibility for the others.

The exchange list included a total of 390 people from the camp at Weihsien. We were put in three coaches on a train bound for Shanghai. Can you imagine 130 people in each coach that should carry 60 to 80 passengers? We thought we were packed like sardines, but we were not! We found out later what it was really like.

The Japanese officials told us that, normally, it would take two days to get to Shanghai, but because of the war, it might take three. Actually, it took four.

Three times before we reached Nanking, the train ahead of us was blown up by guerrillas. They were not aiming at us; they were just destroying Japanese property which had been confiscated from the Chinese during the Japanese occupation. The Lord saw to it that it was not our train that was blown up. We had to wait hour after hour while they cleared away the wreckage, repaired the track and sent us on through.

While we waited we were allowed to walk alongside the train. There were always armed guards to keep us from escaping. "Escape from going home?" I thought. "Who would want to escape?" But then I heard of one man in the group who was under indictment for the murder of his wife before he left the States. He would be apprehended and punished as soon as he landed. No wonder he tried to escape. Another man, while sleeping, had a bad dream and tried to run away. What a mercy he was captured and returned, not shot.

Finally we reached Nanking. There we were told, "So sorry! Your train has gone."

I didn't think it had. There was a train sitting there, its engine steamed up, ready to go.

They roped off an area for us. It was a hot sultry day in August. I've never seen anything hotter or more sultry anywhere in the southern states, USA, than it was there that day.

We stood around there for hours. Along about noon, Mr. Koga, the Japanese officer in charge, started handing out some loaves of bread, not nice, long, sliced loaves neatly wrapped in plastic bags, but chunks of bread and not wrapped at all. This was our third day on the road. If we had any of our lunch left, with no refrigeration, it was unfit to eat. We were grateful for this supply of bread.

Mr. Koga had just handed out a few chunks of bread when suddenly a railroad official came running up. They held a hurried conversation. Immediately, Mr. Koga shouted, "No more bread! Everyone on the train!"

We got on that already steamed up train just as fast as we could, through doors and windows, anything to get on. As the train began to move, I saw Mr. Koga, who was in the same coach, look at his watch. "I didn't believe it was possible!" he exclaimed. Seven and one-half minutes from the time he had received the order, the train was in motion. We had left neither a stick nor a thread behind.

Nanking was bombed a few minutes later. The Japanese knew the planes were coming. That was why they were hurrying us out. At that time, we were very important people. Each of us was worth one Japanese prisoner of war. If anything happened to one of us, the whole exchange would fall through.

We quickly got away from Nanking and sped down the tracks. Soon we were in the territory near Yangchow where I had gone to language school seven years earlier. I began to think, "Oh, we'll soon be in Shanghai and we'll get a chance to get off and rest."

We stopped again and just sat! I wondered, "Has another train been blown up? Can we stand it if we have to wait here while more wreckage is cleared away?" But there was nothing else we could do.

Soon some officials came along and said, "There is fighting on the line ahead."

We knew we were in the fighting zone, but we didn't know how near to the actual fighting. Finally, the railroad officials got out and changed the signs on the outside of the coaches to read from "TO SHANGHAI" to "TO NANKING." They put the engine on the other end of the train and started back.

Those who had been due to come out the year before on the exchange which had fallen through, could imagine themselves going clear back to the concentration camp, and there were tears. Some of us had not been included the other time and didn't know enough to fear return to camp. We just thought we were on our way home to the States.

For a while our train rolled back rapidly, then they shoved our coaches onto a sidetrack beside three carloads of squealing pigs. There we spent the night in **good company**. The next morning they joined the engine onto the pig train, hooked us on behind, and took the "PIG AND AMERICAN SPECIAL" on to Shanghai without a stop. We should have been offended that the pigs had precedence over us, but it didn't bother us. We were on our way home!

In Shanghai we got off and had to stand and wait to be counted. We waited and waited while they decided what to do with us. They knew where they were to take us, but not how. They could not make up their minds whether to move us by train or by bus.

They finally put us on busses and took us out, about a twenty minute trip, to beautiful, grassy St. John's University campus. They kept ten or twelve of our men and older boys to handle the luggage so it wouldn't take so many busses.

We were so tired that we had been saying, "Nothing is going to keep us from lying down!"

Just then a Japanese guard came along and said, "There is food in the dining room for you."

We promptly forgot all about the desire to rest.

We rushed to the improvised dining room and had a meal of just plain Irish stew, plain bread with nothing to spread on it, plain tea with no milk or sugar; but nothing ever tasted better! It was our first hot food in four days. When we got the same thing that night, it wasn't quite as interesting. And when they warmed it up again for breakfast the next morning, some began to grumble. It was still food, wasn't it? And it was hot!

After the first hot meal, we still had thoughts of resting, but the Japanese had other ideas. No resting was allowed.

About two or three hours later when the men and boys had not yet arrived with our luggage, we became quite concerned. When they did catch up with us, they told us that we had not been ten minutes out of the station when a time bomb had exploded right where we had been standing. Nothing had happened to them or to any of our things. It was just red tape that had delayed them. Wasn't it gracious of the Lord to let us know how He had arranged for our protection?

(Skeptics would say, "Wasn't it lucky you came through when nothing was happening?" Nothing happening? It happened right before us! It happened right behind us! The Lord just took us through safely. We could not fail to see that it was His doing!)

That night at the University campus, we slept on folding army cots which broke very easily and not because of our weight or carelessness. I never saw such brittle wood. I told the girls to sit back on the beds and not put their weight on the wooden cross-pieces. In the middle of the night, I awoke and sat up quickly, forgetting the necessity of keeping my weight evenly distributed. Of course, a wooden leg snapped and for the rest of the night I had to prop my bed on my suitcase.

The next morning we left for the prison ship. As usual, all luggage must be inspected. The Japanese inspected everything my seven girls and I had. We unlocked the girls' suitcases one by one. Each girl took her turn holding all the keys and identification papers while I repacked her luggage.

When it came time to open my suitcase, for some reason we could not find the keys. Nobody knew which girl had them last. We looked and looked for them, but still no keys. The Japanese inspector was getting more and more impatient. I tried to borrow a key, but could find nothing to fit. At last I found one key that turned the lock.

That inspector, convinced I had something I was trying to hide, went through everything I had with a **fine-toothed comb**. He was so angry with me that he threw everything I had out in the center of the floor in the midst of the milling crowd. I was completely mortified and had to squat in the middle of the floor to repack my suitcase.

The keys finally came to light several days later, on board the Teia Maru, in a basket belonging to a lady who, possibly, had been standing beside us in the inspection line. Who dropped them in? Perhaps one of the children, by accident, or it may be that the inspector himself had accidentally picked them up and dropped them in.

C·H·A·P·T·E·R 18

THE TEIA MARU

After almost endless difficulties, we boarded the prison ship, the Teia Maru, an old French boat that had been taken by the Japanese and reconditioned. And what a condition! The normal capacity was 400-500 passengers. There were nearly 1600 of us. We knew now how sardines were packed, only they were dead and we were not — yet.

The sleeping quarters for the women and girls were on the main deck. Each had a straw tick, sort of a mattress cover stuffed with grass, weeds and roots — quite lumpy and not at all comfortable. They were about six feet long and anywhere from fifteen to twenty-four inches wide. (I measured some of them.) They were jammed together side by side, as close as could be, thirty-five in a row. Just to make it interesting, my number was eighteen; there were seventeen people on each side of me. There was another "shelf" about eighteen inches above us with its thirty-five people. There definitely was not enough room to sit up. There was just barely enough room to slither into your space.

Another thirty-five people had their heads next to ours, and there were thirty-five more above them. At their feet and our feet were aisles just barely wide enough to walk through and more shelves for more people. There were 240 of us in that one enclosed deck space. Our sleeping quarters were hot and steamy with hardly any light and no air circulation.

The men and the boys had similar accommodations down in the hold of the ship where there was even less air circulation.

The old, the feeble, the sick and a few "especially favored" ones had cabin accommodations.

One of the senior missionaries was ill and was given a cabin. One day a friend came in to tidy her cabin. The missionary had left her dentures in a tin can full of water. The woman who was cleaning picked up the can and threw the water, with the teeth, through the porthole into the ocean. She heard the teeth clink just as the water left the can. Now the poor lady had no teeth. What could she do?

A notice was posted on the bulletin board: "Does anybody have extra dentures?" (People who travel often carry an extra set in case one breaks.)

An elderly Southern Baptist pastor, a missionary, had a set of teeth, which with just a little adaptation, would fit her. (There were dentists and doctors on board who were also prisoners. They had nothing to work with, but looked after the prisoners' needs the best they could.) One of these dentists was able to make the necessary adjustments, and so the lady had teeth the rest of the way home.

There were not enough deck chairs to accommodate the passengers. Perhaps there were one hundred chairs but there were about 1600 people to use them! My girls and I usually sat on the deck on my steamer rug (blanket), the only place available.

We could get drinking water twice a day, for one-half hour in the morning and again for one-half hour in the afternoon – if it wasn't forgotten.

Living conditions were horrible. Flies were always buzzing around the food on the dining tables and we had no swatters to knock them down. They congregated in swarms in the restrooms. There were flush toilets, but not nearly enough for the number of passengers. That, with an insufficient water supply, made the restrooms extremely filthy.

There were so few wash basins and so little water for so many people that there was no chance for a decent bath, not even a **canary bath**. We sort of dry cleaned ourselves, which may have been a better policy anyway.

The water shortage made it especially hard to keep the children clean. I often heard the lady in charge of the little boys ask, "Did you wash your face this morning?"

"No."

"Why not?"

"There wasn't any water."

"Did you think of using sea water?"

"No, I didn't think of that."

As for laundry facilities, there were none. We could rinse out a garment or two in sea water and hang it wherever we could find space enough.

There were many humorous things that

happened and the Lord enabled us to laugh and enjoy them. It was by no means all funny but the Lord provided enough humor to balance the ugly, rugged part and make the experience bearable.

The Japanese crew had many boxes of saki, (their rice wine) stowed away in the hold of the ship. Some of the passengers found that store of saki and were slick enough to steal some without being caught. The Japanese authorities were quite furious about it. They could not catch them stealing; they could only catch them drunk.

Strangely enough, there was no seasickness on board the Teia Maru. The seas were as calm as could be most of the time, even though it was the stormy season. It had to be the hand of the Lord intervening on our behalf. He has promised that the testing will never be greater than we can bear.

There were four classes of dining rooms, three sittings (or shifts) for each meal. My seven girls and I were fortunate enough to eat in the first class dining room at the second sitting. The lady who occupied my chair at the first sitting was one of the few who still had some lipstick. She always left a little ring of it on the glass. The glasses were never washed between servings and I was able to see which side of the glass had been used. I didn't like to look at that little ring, so I rubbed it off. The poor fellow who sat there at the next sitting wouldn't know which side had been used and which had not.

At mealtime they gave us each a small juice glass with about three inches of water in it. It was all yours, you could have it all if you wanted it; but they never refilled it for you. If you only took part of it, they did not empty the glass; they brought it up to that same level for the next person. Water was scarce and must not be wasted. For anyone who appreciates cleanliness, that was rough.

We commonly referred to our food as our "Lutheran Diet." You will recall that Martin Luther was tried by the Diet of Worms. So were we! To Luther, a Diet was a court; Worms was a city in Germany. But it was neither court nor city to us. Our rice was thoroughly wormy. You could eat it or leave it. You know, when you're really hungry, you eat what is set before you; and we were hungry. After all, that was the only fresh meat we had!

Once it was reported to the captain of the ship that over 500 prisoners were down with dysentery. "Don't you know you should expect that?" he said. "We're crossing the equator!"

We crossed the equator three more times and it never happened again.

The stewards on the ship knew that we had been allowed to bring along a little money. Down a shadowy corridor, a Japanese steward might offer one a cup of coffee for ten dollars. Someone might clean your cabin for ten dollars. Otherwise, the cabins were never cleaned. There was just no service at all; but then I suppose one shouldn't expect service on a prison ship!

There was a shortage of bread, but we could buy a slice of bread and butter down the corridor at night for five dollars. Occasionally, fruit was sold the same way. We were all hungry.

I arranged to buy one loaf of bread each day for ten dollars for the girls in my care. Another lady and her daughters had some spread, but no bread.

We combined our resources and one loaf of bread made a snack for twelve people every day.

Three days before the end of the journey, the Japanese said, "No more bread." Nothing was available even though it had been paid for in advance. So we twelve were hungrier each afternoon.

We were often too hungry to sleep at night. On the Teia Maru we got so thin that when we met the American Medical Authorities as we boarded the Gripsholm they said we were the largest group of the most emaciated Americans they had ever seen. They may have seen worse later, but we were, indeed, a sight to behold!

We were on the Teia Maru for one full month. Ordinarily, the distance would have been covered in much less time. It was wartime; the seas were all mined – explosive devices were hidden under the water to destroy enemy ships. Troopships had mine sweepers, devices to locate and remove mines, but the Teia Maru did not. We had to use untraveled routes and that made a big difference both in time and distance.

At each port, we stopped and picked up more prisoners as we traveled from Shanghai down to Hong Kong, across to San Fernando in the Philippine Islands, up through the Mekong River to Saigon, back and through the Straits of Java, over to Mormugoa, a Portuguese port on the west coast of India.

At Mormugoa we were to meet the Gripsholm, the Swedish-American ship which was to take us the rest of the way home to the States. The hulls of sunken ships in the harbor were a grim reminder that a war was going on.

When we arrived at Mormugoa on the fifteenth of October, the Gripsholm wasn't there. I'm afraid those who had been disappointed before could see us going all the way back to camp and there were tears again. They were sure they could not survive another month of what they had just been through, and they possibly could not have.

But we docked, and the next morning the big, beautiful Gripsholm came in around the rocks and they tied it up right in front of us. The Teia Maru was much taller and narrower than the Gripsholm, so we looked down on her.

As the Gripsholm was docking, the Japanese on that ship, who were to be exchanged for us, sang their national anthem. The tones had not died away before somebody on the Gripsholm began to sing **"God Bless America."** We had never heard that song before, but we could understand some of the words, and we wondered who could be singing for us.

It seems that the ship, when ready to leave New York, was short of crew members. An appeal was sent out on the east coast for young men who were not in any branch of the service to come help bring us home in safety. It was this little group of American boys and the ship's crew that was singing for us.

We were on the high ship. Naturally, our youngsters had crowded as far forward as they could to see everything that was going on. When the music ended, they called down to those people on the Gripsholm: "What have you got to eat on your ship?"

Oh, we heard a long list – a lot of things we had not allowed ourselves to think about for a long time. You know, when you're a little bit hungry, you talk about mealtime. When you get more hungry, you don't talk about it, but you think about it. When you get really hungry, you don't allow yourself even to think about food, for it brings on those awful hunger pangs. We had not allowed ourselves to think about those things for a long, long time. Then those on the Gripsholm made a horrible mistake.

They called to our youngsters, "What do you want to eat?" They got the same list back with a few extras added. Then those extravagant Americans began to throw fruit up, trying to reach us on our deck. Some of it fell into the sea. That was awfully hard to bear. We were so hungry for it.

We stayed on the Teia Maru for three days while they stowed Red Cross parcels containing emergency food supplies and clothing in the hold of the Teia Maru for those prisoners who were still in the prison camp. We had never seen a Red Cross parcel while we were in camp because, during the previous exchange, when the Japanese passengers were all aboard, away that ship went, leaving all our Red Cross parcels in Madagascar in South Africa. But now our friends who were still in the camp would have the benefit of the food and clothing in those parcels.

CHAPTER 19

THE LUXURIOUS GRIPSHOLM

At last we were ready to make the actual exchange. We walked off the Teia Maru along the dock to the nearest port on the Gripsholm. The Japanese came out of another port of the Gripsholm and walked along the dock a distance from us to a further port of the Teia Maru. We were far enough apart that we could not see the individuals for whom we were being exchanged. It was just so many Americans in exchange for an equal number of Japanese.

The Japanese coming off the Gripsholm were wearing beautiful American clothing and carrying handsome American luggage. They looked like tourists.

Our luggage was falling apart; so were we and our clothing, too. All in all we looked like the prisoners that we were. But, do you know, we were sorry for those Japanese! Many of them were college and university students who had been studying in America and did not want to go back home to war-torn Japan. A few of those Japanese, we were told, were keen Christians in poor health who chose to go in order to spend their remaining days telling their people about the Lord Jesus Christ.

I don't know how it was decided who should go, but we knew they were going to poverty stricken, war-torn Japan and would lose everything they had. They could not go into Japan like tourists with all those lovely things.

But we were coming home to America and we knew that things would be very different from what we had been experiencing as prisoners of the Japanese. We were so grateful to God for it!

(If you have no appreciation for America, just visit another country for a while, even for a few hours, and you'll come back here grateful for what God has done for us and our country. Of course, there are many things wrong here, but we have so much to be grateful for and so much for which to thank God.)

Soon the Japanese were high up on the Teia Maru looking down at us on the Gripsholm. There were a few Christians on each ship, but they were far in the minority. The two groups of Christians, though on separate ships, drew closer and together sang **"Jesus shall reign where'er the sun doth his successive journeys run,"** and **"In Christ there is no east or west – in Him no south or north."** There is a unity among Christians even though they are separated by war and distance.

Then one of the Japanese prisoners on the Teia Maru called out to us, "When you get back to Washington (D.C.), won't you see what you can do so the next group of Japanese can have their Bibles? There's not a Bible on this ship."

They couldn't understand why the Americans had taken their Bibles. We couldn't understand that either. Our Bibles had been inspected; we lost all our marked, familiar study Bibles. I had been given a little American Revised Version with my name halfway down the flyleaf. The inspectors had torn that flyleaf off and let me have my Bible back, so I had a Bible, though many did not.

When we got back to the States, we found that, apparently, an American inspector looking through the Japanese Bibles, checking for marks, just as the Japanese had done in ours, spotted a Japanese code book passing for a Bible. Who knew how many more there might be? So they called in all the Bibles.

The American Bible Society offered a new Japanese Bible for every prisoner on board, but those officials in charge of propaganda said, "No! The Americans took our Bibles!" And the prisoners didn't know why their Bibles had been taken away.

Ours could easily have been taken away for the same reason. I went out on deck one day and there sat a "missionary" with a **Complete Works of Shakespeare** around which she had put a Bible cover. (She thought more of Shakespeare than she did of her Bible.) If the inspectors had discovered that it wasn't a Bible, we could all have lost ours – just as the Japanese did. When rules are made it doesn't pay to disregard them.

What a contrast there was between the ship we had just left and the one we were on now! The Gripsholm was a luxury liner. After the deplorable conditions of the Teia Maru, she was, to us, the ultimate in luxury. The crew showed real friendliness; they were all as kind and helpful as could be.

The Gripsholm was roomy, luxurious and beautifully clean. The **crew** complained about the crowded conditions. Cabins with two berths had become cabins with four berths. My seven girls were now in two cabins near each other. We were very comfortable after the **doubtful comforts** of the Teia Maru. The berths were a welcome change from the knotty straw ticks we had endured on the other ship. We had everything we needed and we praised the Lord for it all!

We had our first meal on the Gripsholm while she was still in port. They served us white bread that was really white. We couldn't believe our eyes. Our white bread in China had been so dark. To us this looked like angel food cake. We thought they surely wouldn't serve us cake so soon after we had been so hungry for such a long time!

The dietitians, knowing we had been nutritionally deprived for a long time, carefully provided for our needs. It was a real treat to have good food, clean dishes and plenty of water. We all enjoyed the well balanced, carefully planned and supervised meals. The government provided vitamins to help build up our bodies, and doctors to treat whatever medical needs we might have. What luxury!

At last the ship began to move. When we were a legally prescribed distance out to sea, we were given our mail, our first in two years! The newspapers in America had published lists of passengers, prisoners from their areas, who were coming home, and where, and when, they might receive mail. So our families and friends had written to us. How wonderful it was to hear from our loved ones, yet so heartbreaking to learn of those who had been lost in the war.

Our first port of call as free people was Port Elizabeth in South Africa. For two days, we were allowed to take short walks about the city.

As we wandered through the streets, to our delight, we came upon a Woolworth store – a touch of home! We walked in and began to look around. Imagine our surprise when the management of those stores presented us with small bags of hard candies! That treat was truly appreciated. We had almost forgotten what candy was like!

After two weeks of carefully supervised diet on the Gripsholm, we looked better. Yet, many people we met on the street asked, "Are you from the ship?" (They didn't need to ask; they could see how malnourished we had been.)

We would answer, "Yes."

"We've been praying for you," was their reply.

What a bond there is among believers! They did not know us at all, but they had been praying for our safety and God had answered their prayers.

From Port Elizabeth, we went around the tip of South Africa and up to Brazil. Our next port of call was Rio de Janeiro, said to be the most beautiful harbor in the world. Everyone eagerly looked forward to seeing it, but we found ourselves peering into a dense bank of fog. We could not see a thing, but suddenly the clouds parted. We looked up to the top of Mount Corcovado near Sugar Loaf Mountain. In the sunlight stood the statue of the Living Christ with arms outstretched. It was an impressive sight and a hush fell over even the Godless in the crowd. In just a moment the clouds drifted back together and we went on into the harbor in the darkness of dense fog.

Missionaries from other mission groups were talking about their people who were coming from Latin American countries to meet them in Rio. Since we were from the China Inland Mission which, naturally, had no workers in this part of the world we were not expecting anyone to meet us. We had decided we would have a good time by ourselves. When we went downstairs to lunch, however, there in front of my plate was a note.

"Dear Miss Philips," I read. "I am an old Chefoo boy. My wife and I live here in Rio. We would like to entertain the Chefoo people while you are here."

When we walked off the ship, there was our old Chefoo boy with his wife and two young sons. (He had finished school at Chefoo before my arrival and now was in charge of General Electric in Rio.) He and his family took us everywhere they could to show us the sights. The fog was so thick we couldn't see the beauty, but we felt it.

That evening our new friends took our group out to their home for supper. Our hostess had found all the things Chefoo children liked, including peanut butter. They served our whole crowd, about forty of us – both children and adults. Then our host showed slides he had taken in different parts of Latin America.

Afterward, he gave his testimony. He said, "Now, when you get home, young folks, take a firm stand. Don't compromise. When you begin to compromise is when trouble begins."

That was good advice to give those children who were going home without their parents – for they could not join their parents on the mission field in

China. This was an American exchange and they must plant their feet on American soil.

The next day when we left Rio, the sun was shining. It was a beautiful day and we could see some of the beauty we could only feel the day before.

P·A·R·T 6

OUR GOD IS FAITHFUL

C·H·A·P·T·E·R

BACK TO THE STATES
1943

After two weeks on untraveled routes in the Atlantic Ocean we entered the mouth of the Hudson River in New York State. As the ship steamed up the river, everyone was eagerly looking forward to seeing the Statue of Liberty. As time went by with no sight of her, some began to suggest, "We must have missed her in the night fog."

A spirit of disappointment fell over us until suddenly a voice shouted, "There she is! The Statue of Liberty!"

We dashed to the side of the ship so we could see her standing there holding up her light to welcome us home. How exciting it was! As we went on up the river, people on ferries and other boats shouted to us. What a thrill we all felt as we heard the blowing of horns and greetings of people eagerly welcoming us home. A little later (about 9:00 A.M.) we docked in New York City Harbor.

We had been given long questionnaires to

This photo and caption appeared in the New York Evening Gazette:
GRIPSHOLM BRINGS FREEDOM TO 1500
New York, Dec. 1.—The diplomatic exchange ship Gripsholm, carrying fifteen hundred Americans interned by Japan nearly two years ago, pushing up the North River and past the Statue of Liberty this morning on the way to a berth in Jersey City. Each passenger was questioned by FBI and other agents before being allowed to leave the ship. (Associated Press Wirephoto.)

Mission headquarters in Philadelphia where I left the missionary children.

answer to speed the disembarkment procedure. When I reached the desk, I was sent back into a corridor for special questioning. Somewhat shaken, I went down the corridor wondering, "What have I done? Why should I be sent back for special questioning?" I knew there were some known criminals on board who had been allowed to walk off the ship unhindered – but maybe there was someone waiting to take them into custody.

I found all our children down that corridor, also sent back for special questioning. The authorities only wanted to ask them, "Why are you traveling without your parents?"

One of the girls was developing epilepsy. She often had slight petit mal seizures. The stress and strain of the day, plus the strain of the past few years, was too much for her. While we were waiting in the corridor, she had the worst seizure I had ever seen her have. I almost despaired of her ever coming out of it.

What a blessing the Lord had sent me back for special questioning. He knew I would be needed in that corridor. The children, with no adult present, would not have known what to do. The Lord knew what He was doing when He sent me back to be with the children.

Later, I found that someone, apparently, had asked me a question while I was filling out my questionnaire and I had failed to answer this one question: **"Have you ever been in the employ of any other government?"** That omission would be enough to condemn anyone.

It was about 7:30 that evening when I walked off the ship with the last child. A kind gentlemen from another mission had helped me with the children. He sent his family on to the hotel and he received and helped each of my seven girls through customs and kept them together as a unit until I got there. When I came off the ship with the last child, he even helped me. His help was surely appreciated.

We greeted the CIM Mission group and were talking together when someone said, "By the way, Martha, your brother is waiting for you over there."

My doctor brother and his wife from Worcester, Massachusetts had come to meet me! They had been waiting since early that morning. (This brother is just two and one-half years older than I and we were very close.) We were so happy to see each other after so many years! We had a most joyful reunion, though he was shaken and concerned to find me so thin and worn.

He and his wife waited for a day in New York while I took the children to Mission headquarters in Philadelphia and left them there. The children were to remain there until their parents returned to the States and the families could be reunited. They attended various schools, but came back to Mission headquarters to be together at night. To have sent the children to relatives who did not understand the stress they had been under for years would have added to their problems of adjustment. When I returned to New York, my brother and his wife took me on a hurried tour of New York City, then on to their home in Worcester where I stayed for three months to recuperate from malnutrition and stress and to build up my strength. When I was able, they allowed me to go to my parents who now lived in Seattle.

(There were two Phillips children in our Mission – Richard and Kathryn – with two "l"s in their name, whereas mine has only one. Each time the Japanese typed our passenger list, they put my name down, saw the two children's names, rolled the list back, put another "l" in my name and donated me the two children.)

By the time I was ready to go home to Seattle, the Phillips children's parents had reached their home in Portland, Oregon. Mission headquarters asked me, "Would you, please, take the Phillips children to the West Coast with you?"

I agreed, but Kathryn developed the mumps the day before we were to leave for Portland.

"Mumps, again?" I thought, and went to visit my cousin in Berea, Kentucky while I waited for her recovery.

Another CIM missionary brought the children to Chicago, then, where I met them. We were to take a train from there to Portland. Since we would be two days and nights on the train, I felt I needed some washcloths to keep the children clean. I let the youngsters go across the street to a dime store to buy some. They came back some time later, terribly embarrassed, without washcloths.

No one at the store knew what they wanted to buy. It seemed that everyone in the store had gathered around the two **Britishers** who wanted to buy **flannels**.

"What kind of flannels?" they were asked.

"Face flannels," the youngsters answered with a British accent.

"Face flannels? What is that?"

"To wash your face."

"They don't make them anymore. It's wartime, you know."

The clerks laughed in amusement and two embarrassed youngsters rushed from the store.

(When the Americans were leaving Vietnam in 1975, a group of missionaries was taken captive. Two of those captured were Richard and Lillian Phillips. That Richard Phillips was the little boy I had brought home from China. When I heard that he was captured, I thought, "Oh, oh! Richard is getting a review lesson."

Read the book **"Captured"** by Carolyn Miller. When Richard was captured as a child, his parents were up-country in China and he was in school. Now, as a parent in Vietnam, he was captured and his children were away at school.

I haven't had the privilege of seeing him since he came home, but I am sure he has a rich testimony of the Lord's deliverance in Vietnam. He is now serving the Lord in Africa.)

By the time I reached Seattle I had been around the world on a diagonal. We had completed a seventy-five day ocean voyage and at that time I thought I'd never want to see the ocean or a ship again, but I have enjoyed other ocean trips since then. I now know more of the Lord's "Peace, be still." (Mark 4:39) Of all those seventy-five days on the ocean, we could count on the fingers of one hand the number of days we could even see whitecaps. That doesn't just happen, but it did, and it was during the stormy season of the year.

You may never have seen the oily sea that always precedes a typhoon. Seamen say when that happens the typhoon never fails to strike, but none struck where we were. Often when that occurred

I heard somebody say, "Someone's praying!" And we knew it was true, for Christians around the world were praying for our safety and the Lord heard and answered those prayers.

(Don't let anybody tell you that God doesn't hear and answer prayer. I know He does for I have prayed and have seen the Lord's answer. I have also been on the receiving end of other people's prayers on my behalf many times. Just stay in touch with your Heavenly Father, and He will hear and answer your prayers.)

C·H·A·P·T·E·R

A NEW COMMISSION

The Lord's call of "Go ye" still held. I never dreamed of anything but of returning to China. Finally my health was restored. I taught at the University of Washington at Seattle for two years to prove I would not crack up under pressure. During that time the China Inland Mission told me that in returning to China I might go to the tribes of West China.

Like many countries, China has aboriginal tribes, those people who were there first. At the time the China Inland Mission made a survey of the province of Yunnan alone, they found one hundred tribes. One hundred languages! People speaking no Chinese. The only way to reach people is with their own language. I had always been interested in those tribes. In fact, I had hoped to go to them when I first went to China, so I was pleased when the Mission told me that I might go to the tribes.

Then I heard about a group of people who taught what they called "linguistics" – the basic principles of hearing and analyzing languages.

This would prepare me for Bible translation, for teaching of reading and bringing of the Gospel to those who had no written language. That would be helpful in China. So I studied with them and thoroughly enjoyed it. Everyone in Wycliffe Bible Translators knew I was never going to work with them. I was going back to China.

The sailing date was set months in advance, as it always is, but just two weeks before I was to sail, the China door closed. What a bitter disappointment that was!

Whenever the going is rough, Satan is on hand, and he was right there. He said to me, "See! You're finished! What of the life you were going to spend in China? The Lord is through with you. He has put you on the shelf. There's nothing more you can do. You're too old to do anything else for Him."

When I finally recognized the source of the problem, I turned to the Lord and said, "Lord, I thought it was China. But what I've really done is to give myself to You. Now, what do You want me to do? Where do you want me to go?"

He indicated Mexico.

"Mexico?" I asked. "That's not much of a mission field! They are just our next door neighbors." But our next door neighbors are a mission field, aren't they?

Then the thought came to me, "They all talk Spanish. I don't know any Spanish – but I might learn it!"

I soon learned they don't all talk Spanish. I went with Wycliffe the next year (1950) on a loan basis expecting China to reopen. That door has not yet opened, and I have been working with

Wycliffe since 1950.

At the time Wycliffe Bible Translators went down into Mexico, we were told there were fifty tribes of Indians there. Fifty tribes with none of God's Word in writing! That meant we would have to do fifty New Testaments for Mexico. We thought that was quite a challenge, but we undertook it.

Today we are working with about 130 languages in Mexico, and there are at least twenty we haven't gotten into yet. The government was not aware how many languages there were. Over 81 New Testaments in various Indian languages in Mexico were completed by 1988 and put into the hands of the people.

(The need for translation worldwide is mind-boggling. There are over 3,000 more language groups that do not have the Scripture.)

Many of those people in Mexico have heard John 3:16 in Spanish and it doesn't mean a thing to them, but when they hear it in their own language, they can understand it.

We rejoice to hear one of them say, "Oh, is that what it means? It is just like God is talking to me."

Isn't that what God's Word is to us? Aren't you glad He talks to you and to me? Aren't you glad that back in the fourteenth century when there was none of God's Word in English, one man in England was concerned for the poor heathen English speaking people?

The only ones who could read the Bible in those days were those who could read Hebrew, Greek or Latin. The common people had no opportunity for that kind of education.

John Wycliffe started translating the Word of God into English. After his death, William Tyndale took on the work. Wycliffe, Tyndale and others laid down their lives to give the Word of God to us in our own language.

When Wycliffe Bible Translators was ready to choose a name, what better name to choose than that of the man who had first begun translating the Bible for us?

Don't go to the mission field just because it is thrilling. If you go for that reason only, the thrills will wear out and soon you will say, "Why did I come here anyway? Maybe I misread the signals and it was my choice, not God's."

Others may already be asking those questions. The important thing is to deal with the Lord Jesus Christ. If you know what He wants and you are in the place of His choosing, you will be able to take what He sends and know that "God is still on the throne."

Sometimes it may be very rough. I did not choose concentration camp. I would not take anything in exchange for the experience of proving my God; but I tell you, I would not choose to go back into it either. Wherever God sends you, He'll meet your needs for He is faithful. Don't ever forget that. Be sure, whatever you take up, that you are doing what the Lord is asking you to do. He wants to be definite, not leave us in uncertainty.

In facing the problems ahead, you might say, "I could not do that." You can't, but God can do it through you. Remember, it is not one's wonderful personality or intelligence that does the work; it is our wonderful Lord who calls us and makes us able. If you want a place of joy, a life of real joy and peace, find where the Lord wants you and get yourself there as soon as possible. Don't let anything interfere, for that is the place of real joy and peace.

As long as we have life and breath the Lord has work for us. It may not be in a public ministry, but the hidden work of prayer is most important. Everyone of us can, and should, pray for the missionaries and those they are trying to reach, as well as for those in the mission field around us. Pray earnestly, pray diligently. God has promised to answer; He will answer, for God always keeps His promises.

We are not all called to the foreign field – the field is the world, and that includes your own home and neighborhood. We are all called to work for the Lord.

Where is your place of service? What work has God planned for you? Are you in that place? Remember, delayed obedience is disobedience!

"He cannot fail for He is God.
He cannot fail, He's pledged His Word.
He cannot fail; He'll see you through,
'Tis God with whom we have to do."

Our Father, we do thank You that You are our Father. We thank You that no testing that comes our way can touch us without Your permission. And when it comes with Your permission, it comes as a message of love from You. Our Father, we pray that You'll send to us what we need to make us strong in You, and that You'll meet the need of each one. Help us to desire, above all else, to please You. And Father, we take a moment now to pray for those Chinese people in Chefoo who have not known a day of peace since 1938. Lord, we don't know how many Christians are left there, but we know that You are not defeated and we pray that many more might come to know You there. We pray, too, that You'll send the gospel to the Communists in some way. We don't know how, we leave it in Your hands.

We thank You, Lord, for the privilege of knowing You and ask that You help us to be faithful to You. In Jesus' Name. Amen.